OUR NAMES

Where They Came From and What They Mean

OUR NAMES

WHERE THEY CAME FROM
AND WHAT THEY MEAN

BY ELOISE LAMBERT
AND MARIO PEI

LOTHROP, LEE & SHEPARD CO.

NEW YORK

8   9   10   75   74   73   72   71

Contents

Part III: THING NAMES

OUR NAMES

Where They Came From and What They Mean

Introduction

"What's your name?"

In the very beginning of an acquaintance, this is a natural first question. But it is really several questions in one. The answer will often give you a clue as to the speaker's racial or national origin. But be careful. With a first name the clue is often deceptive, and even with the family name the indications are sometimes misleading.

In some ways the personal name goes deep into the mental processes of the group that uses it, though it does not tell you too much about the group's external history. If you trace back carefully, you may be able to get some valuable leads about the religious beliefs of the users, the fund of traditional folklore at their disposal, the qualities they consider important, the terms of endearment or derision they use. It will show you something of how their minds work.

The family name, where it exists, will give a fair indication of locations, occupations, and trades. It will often be a clear clue to the nationality or race of its owner, but it may be distorted or disguised in such a way as to require a great deal of study before it yields its message.

Personal names, being personal, are far more individualistic than place names, which are often officially bestowed, or are the product of mass consultation, or of the choice of a single person in authority. In personal names, both first and family, the human imagination has the freest play, and the results are often fascinating or humorous.

Given a simple, common, everyday name like John Smith, what can you tell by the name alone?

Granting that the name is authentic, and has not been changed from something else, you can at once put together the following facts about its owner: he belongs to an English-speaking group, which may be American, British, Canadian, Australian, or may come from one of the other English-speaking areas; this you know because the form of the name is typically English. If you knew nothing more about English speakers, you would be able, from the name of John Smith, to piece together this information: they are religiously inclined, either Christian or Jewish, and believe in the Bible. (John is a Biblical name, of Hebrew origin, but widely used among all Christians; downright atheists would tend to avoid religious names for their children, and since the name of John is so widespread, the majority of the users of the language in which John appears must be inclined toward religion.) From Smith, you would be able to tell that the users of the name are mechanically inclined, know how to work metals, and, since the name Smith is also widespread, that they have a considerable amount of industrial development. All this happens to be true about English speakers, and it is very common knowledge. But these conclusions were not reached from previous knowledge; they were reached simply from studying the name John Smith.

The same indications would be there in the case of John Smith's Russian counterpart, Ivan Kuznetsov (this name means, literally, John of the Smiths). The indications would also be true of the Russians. The fact that official Soviet circles are atheistically inclined would not be revealed by the name, but the Soviet system of government is, after all, very much of a newcomer in Russian history. For the rest, the clues would be the same save for the big fact that the form Ivan Kuznetsov would at once reveal its possessor to be a member of the Russian, not of the English-speaking, group. So, as we see, the process of observation and deduction is applicable in the case of personal as well as of place names.

There is charm and fascination in knowing what a name means. Certain groups in antiquity, and even some backward people today, believe the knowledge of a person's real name gives power over that person. In a sense this is true, because knowledge of a name gives you the person's identity, the possibility of singling him out from the mass. It is more than likely that personal names, in one form or another, appeared even before place names, for living creatures strike the attention more quickly than their inanimate surroundings.

Personal names lead to other sorts of proper names— names of groups, institutions, organizations of all kinds. No group of individuals, once it is constituted, fails to give itself a name. No corporation is so soulless, or so anonymous (although in some countries a corporation is called an "anonymous society") that it does not bestow a name upon itself. Producers eagerly seek an impressive (or perhaps only a catchy) name for what they produce and try to sell. All sorts of things, from planets to animals, from flowers to chemical elements, become endowed with a personal name, which may be a scientific name, a pet name, a trade name, or even an abbreviated name formed with initials only.

How did the naming fad get started? What is a totem name? To what extent are names descriptive of the people who bear them? What is the role played by race, mythology, religion, in the matter of names? Are names translatable from one language into another? Is a double name really necessary, or will a single name do? These, and many other questions, we shall endeavor to answer in the following pages.

Part I

FIRST NAMES

manic languages give us a broad choice, with Albert, Bernard, Charles, Richard, Robert, Henry, William, Frances, Frederica, Ida. We can be even more specific, and decide from which Germanic branch we want our name; if from Anglo-Saxon, then we have a whole list beginning with *Ed-* (Edward, Edwin, Edmund, Edgar, etc.); if we prefer Scandinavian, then we have Olaf, Norman, Gustave, Kirsten, Hulda, Dagmar, Astrid. French forms, though usually derived from other sources, would be those ending in *-ette*, or *-belle*. Typically Spanish names would be Dolores, Consuelo, Ferdinand, Elvira, Juanita, Alphonse. From Celtic we have a long list that would include Gilda and Genevieve, Rowena and Neil, Morgan, Donald and Duncan. Here, too, we could go specifically Irish with Brian and Colleen, specifically Scottish with Angus, Malcolm and Jessie, specifically Welsh with Evan, Owen and Gwendolyn. We could go Italian with Romola, Francesca and Dino, Russian with Sonya, Boris and Olga, Persian with Cyrus, Darius and Roxana, Sanskrit with Beryl, even American Indian with Wenonah.

Nor should we forget the many and varied possibilities of using the same name in different language forms: John, Jean, Juan, Ian, Ivan, Johann, Sean; or Catherine, Katrina, Cathleen, Karen, Katinka; Agnes or Inez; Roland or Orlando; Charles, Carl, Karl or Carlos. The embarrassment, if any, lies only in the choice.

CHAPTER TWO

Names of Beauty and Derision

If there were ever any names of the type of Ugh and Brr, based on favorite sounds produced by the owner, they are lost in the mists of prehistory. The nearest historical approach we have is the Greek Stentor, whose name derives from the same root that gives us "thunder" (the root word originally meant "loud noise"). Stentor was a man with a very loud voice, and his name has given rise to the adjective "stentorian." The same idea appears today in the family name of one of the top Soviet statesmen, Gromyko, which is built on the Slavic word *grom*, "thunder."

Descriptions of physical characteristics hidden away in first names are quite numerous. Ancient Greek gives us Oedipus, which is "swell-footed." Latin has an entire series: Calvin is "bald," Varus is "bowlegged," Crassus is "fat," Cincinnatus, whose name appears in our city of

Cincinnati, is "curly." Cicero means "chick-pea" or "garbanzo bean," and the name was originally applied because of a wart on the nose of one of Cicero's ancestors. The name Naso itself, one of the names of the Roman poet Ovid, is connected with "nose," and probably meant "long-nosed." Sallust, another Roman poet, bore a name that basically meant "healthy" (we find the root in "salute," "save" and "solid"). Agrippa meant "born feet first." Plautus, like the Greek Oedipus, meant "broad- or flat-footed." Aurelius was "golden," and Dexter was "right-handed." Among color references we find Livy, which seems to mean "bluish," Lucius and Lucian, which go back to the root of "light," Rufus, which is "red," Rosa or Rose, which is "rose" or "rose-colored"; with these goes part of the Celtic Guinevere or Genevieve, which was originally Gwen-hwyfar, "white ghost" or "white enchantress," as well as the French Blanche, "white."

The Celtic Fingal and Dougal go back respectively to Fionn-ghaill ("fair-complexioned stranger") and Dubhghaill ("dark-complexioned stranger"); it is supposed that the first refers to Norwegian, the latter to Danish invaders.

Many other physical qualities are described in names. Cecil and Cecilia both come from the Latin *caecus*, "blind," and originally seem to have meant "dim-sighted" or "one-eyed." Claude, Claudius and Claudia mean "limping" or "lame." Paul is "small" or "little." Seneca, the great orator of ancient Rome, bore a name that meant "old," and is linked with our "senior" and "sire" and with the Spanish *señor*. The same idea occurs in the Germanic

Charles or Karl, with all its variants and feminine forms, such as Charlotte and Carlota; here the root word means "to grow old" or "to become adult," and the meaning was later transferred to "masculine" or "manly"; related words are the German *Kerl* and the Anglo-Saxon *ceorl*, which gives us "churl." The same idea of "manly," "strong," appears in the Roman Nero, the Greek Andrew, and the Persian Cyrus. The originally French Algernon is "bewhiskered," while Belle and Vivien, also from French, mean "beautiful" and "lively," respectively. The second part of Ferdinand is "eager," and Felix is "happy."

Some names bear an indication of the possessor's location or occupation. The Hebrew Malachi, like the Latin Nuntius and the Greek Angelos, which gives us "angel" and Angelo, is "messenger." George is Greek for "farmer," and Philip is "horse-lover." The Celtic Morgan is "seadweller," and Cadwallader, from the same source, is "battle-arranger" or "general." The Hebrew Gideon is "hewer," and the Celtic Orgetorix is "regicide" or "king-killer."

When it comes to qualities that are less physical, Hebrew and Aramaic, the two great languages of the Old Testament, supply us with the best samples. Here we have Noah, "rest" or "comfort"; Abel, "breath" or "vanity"; Ephraim, "fruitful"; Ann, "grace"; Beulah, "married." We also find Judith, "praised"; Solomon, "peaceable"; Seth, "appointed"; Job, "afflicted" or "persecuted"; David, "beloved"; Isaac, "laughter"; and Joseph, which means "he shall add." Greek, too, gives us many descriptive names of the more intellectual or spiritual variety, with Thalia, "blooming"; Sophia, "wisdom";

Philander, "man-loving"; Ambrose and Athanasius, both of which mean "immortal" or "deathless." Both the Greek Eugene and the Celtic Owen (or Yvain, or Eoghan) mean "well-born," and Curtis is the French *courtois*, "courteous," while the Italian Laura, if it doesn't come from *lauro*, "laurel," may go back to *l'aura*, "the air." The Persian Roxana is "dawn," and the Malay Mata Hari is "eye of day" or "sun," thus acting as a perfect parallel for Daisy, or "day's eye."

Hebrew and Aramaic also give us more concrete descriptive names: Adam is "earth," Eve is "life," Abram is "exalted father," Jacob is, in one interpretation, "supplanter," in another "heel" (he is said to have held on to Esau's heel when he was born), while Thomas is "twin." The Greek Barbara means "foreign," the Latin Stella is "star," and Moses seems to come from an ancient Egyptian word meaning "child."

There are a few names that are not very flattering, as we have seen; but their total number is small. Boccaccio, the Italian fourteenth-century writer, bears a name (it was probably a nickname) that means "ugly big mouth." Buffa is Italian for "funny," and Tallulah is claimed to be "terrible" in an American Indian language. Ichabod is Hebrew for "inglorious," and Ulysses is Greek for "hater."

As against these few uncomplimentary forms, the names that exalt their owners are legion. Nobility is portrayed by the Phoenician Hiram ("most noble"), and this idea appears again and again, in the Roman Patrick and Patricia and the Germanic Ethel and Adeline; Earl is an Anglo-Saxon "nobleman." The kingly idea appears in the Greek Basil and in an entire series of names derived from Latin *rex*, "king" (Rex, Roy, Leroy, and the feminine Regina). The French Esmé is "esteemed," the Irish Bridget is "lofty," the Roman Camilla is "free-born," the Germanic Amelia is "industrious." Stephen is a "crown," Samson is derived from the sun, Ethan is "strength," and Alice is "truth." Honora and Honorius have to do with honor, and Eulalie is "fair of speech." Baldwin is "bold friend," Raymond is "wise protection," Archibald is both "noble and bold." The Anglo-Saxon Athelstan is a "noble stone," and his Hebrew counterpart, Ebenezer, is a "stone or rock of help," while the Greek Peter is "rock," without qualification.

The idea of rulership appears quite frequently. Richard is a "strong ruler," Theodoric the "people's ruler," Walter the "ruler of the host," Donald a "world ruler." Fame, too, appears: Roland is "fame of the land," Roderic "rich in fame," Robert "bright in fame" (all names ending in -*bert*, including the plain Bertha, contain this element of brightness; -*bert* and "bright" are in fact the same word).

Warfare and prowess therein are expressed by the Greek Hector, the Latin Martial, and an entire series of Germanic names that celebrate battle, like Hedwig, Hilda ("battle maiden"), Mathilda ("heroine"), William ("resolute helmet"), Herman ("army man"), Herbert ("glory of the host"), Louis and Luther ("famous warrior"), Guy ("leader") and Harold ("army leader"), along with the Celtic Duncan ("brown warrior"). Victory in battle is commemorated by the Roman Victor and Victoria, the Greek Eunice ("fair victory") and Nicholas ("victorious host"), and all Germanic names beginning with *Sieg-* or *Sig-* (Sigmund, Siegfried, etc.)

One last type of descriptive name is the one that contains a numeral, generally indicative of the order in which the holder of the name was born. Here we have the Latin Una ("one"), Quinctus ("fifth"), Sextus ("sixth"), Octavius or Octavian ("eighth"), or a Spanish name like Primo (today the word means "cousin" or "first cousin," but in origin it meant "first"). A similar practice on the other side of the globe appears in Japan, where children are often numbered instead of named: Ichiko, for example, means "number one child," or "firstborn."

Something similar is done by the Ashanti tribes of Ghana, West Africa, who occasionally name their children, from the second on, in the order in which they are born: Manu, Mensah, Anan ("Second," "Third," "Fourth," etc.), up to Badu, "Tenth." But the Ashanti have another and somewhat unique custom, duplicated probably only by Robinson Crusoe when he named his Man Friday. They name their children according to the day of the week on which they are born. The Ashanti days of the week, Sunday through Saturday, are: Kwesiada, Dwoada, Benada, Wukuada, Yawada, Fiada, Memenada. Male children born on each of these days will be named respectively: Kwasi, Kwadwo, Kwabena, Kwaku, Yaw, Kofi and Kwame; females will instead bear the names of Akosua, Adwoa, Abena, Akua, Yaa, Afia, Amma. A second name then tells the child's story. Tawia means "child born after the first set of twins"; Ata means "twin"; Panyin means "elder"; Kuma means "younger." Kofi Buo,

"Friday who has come again," is a second male child born on Friday after the first child born on Friday died. Other "second" names include Nyankomago, "born after the second set of twins," and Tuakosen, "born after the third set of twins." This is description with a vengeance.

CHAPTER THREE

Totem, Animal and Racial Names

With or without the totemic element (that is, the adoption by the tribe of a certain animal to represent it), animal names are of rather frequent occurrence. The American Indians, the Eskimos, the natives of Siberia, and other primitive groups made and still make abundant use of such names. Sitting Bull, the man who defeated Custer, is an excellent example. Another is the Mexican Aztec Netzahualcoyotl, "hungry coyote." That the Romans were addicted to similar names is shown by Catullus, a famous poet, whose name means "cat cub" or "kitten," as well as by various forms taken by the name of "lion" (Leo, Leonidas, Lionel, etc.). Ursus and Lupus, "bear" and "wolf," were commonly bestowed names among the ancient Romans, and France is studded with towns bearing such names as Saint Loup, Saint Leu, or Saint Lô, all of which mean "Saint Wolf." This does not mean that the wolf was saintly or sainted, but merely that someone whose name was Lupus became a saint. Ursula, "little she-bear," is still a current feminine name, and there is even an order of Catholic nuns called the Ursulines after their founder, Saint Ursula.

It was the Germanic tribes, however, who had the real cult of fierce animals, and show it by some of their personal names. Adolf or Adolph is "noble wolf," Rudolph is "red wolf," Arnold is "strong as an eagle," Bernard is "bold or hardy as a bear," Bertram is "bright raven," and Eberhard is "strong as a wild boar." The Germanic-speaking tribes even went to the point of bestowing the name of Wolfgang, or "wolf's tread," as a personal name, and Mozart, the famous composer, was among those who bore it.

The Hebrews, in their Old Testament names, display a good deal of animal preference, but with them it does not seem to have been so much totemic as descriptive or imaginative, and their animal names are usually of the tame and gentle variety. Deborah in Hebrew, like Melissa in Greek, is a "bee," Rachel is "ewe," Tabitha is "gazelle" (the same name appears in Greek under the form Dorcas). Jonah is a "dove," and perhaps the only animal names from Hebrew to which unpleasant connotations could be attached are Caleb, "dog," and Huldah, which means "weasel," and is not to be confused with another Hulda, or Hilda, from Germanic, which means "battle-maiden."

From the totemic animal name it is only a step to the name that indicates race or nationality. Here the ancient Greek world supplies us with a fair sprinkling, including

Lydia and Delia ("from the country of Lydia," in Asia Minor, and "from the island of Delos"), along with Persis, "Persian woman." The Romans give us Sabina ("Sabine woman"), while from Hebrew we get Magdalene ("woman from Magdala"), along with the masculine Israel, which is the name of the tribe. The name Roman is occasionally used today, but there is little evidence that the Romans used it themselves. The Germanic tribes, however, used many of their group names as first names for individuals, and the best-known of these is Frank (the Franks were the Germanic tribe that invaded Roman Gaul and turned it into present-day France). Frank has numerous variants (Francis, the French François, the Italian Francesco, the German Franz, the Spanish Francisco), along with feminine forms like Frances and Francesca. But Frank was by no means the only racial name bequeathed to us by the Germanic tribes. The Alans gave us Allan and Allen, the Saxons gave us Saxon and Sax, the Northmen gave us Norman. The name Lorraine for a girl goes back to the name of the province on the Franco-German border which was once Lotharingia, the region of Lothaire or Luther. It is curious that the Romans, who did not make use of Romanus as a name, did make use of the surname Germanicus, applied by a Roman emperor to the conqueror of the western portion of Germany.

One of the oldest racial names is Arius or Aryus. It holds the same root, meaning "forth from within," that appears in Aryan, Éire, Alan, and the old Germanic tribe of the Alemanni, from whom the French got their generic name for the Germans, *Allemands.*

There is one interesting mixture in the field of national names, that of a painter who became famous in Spain and was surnamed El Greco, "the Greek." He actually came from Crete, which at least partly justifies the surname, since Crete is a Greek-speaking island. But the name has the Spanish definite article, *el*, followed by the Italian, not the Spanish word for "Greek" (*Griego* would be the Spanish). This mixup was probably due to the fact that the painter received his education in Italy before coming to Spain.

cury, Mars and Hermes (the Greek variant of the Roman Mercury).

Other mythological names do not survive quite so well as up-to-date personal names, but they have connections with some very common words. Jupiter, or Jove (his name in Greek was Zeus), was the chief god of the Graeco-Roman Olympus. His root word is *dei-*, "to shine bright," and from it come such forms as the Latin Julius, which gives us July, and *deus*, the general Latin name for God (Jupiter was really a contracted form of *deus pater*, "God the Father"). In Scandinavian form, the root appears not in the name of Odin, the chief Norse god, but in that of *Tīg* or *Tȳr*, the god of war, whose name is embalmed in our Tuesday. Jupiter's wife, queen of the gods, was Juno in the Latin version, Hera in the Greek. The first of these two names is from the same root for "young" that gives us "juvenile," "junior" and "young" itself. The second goes back to a root word that means "to guard or protect"; it appears also in "hero" and "conserve."

Mars, the Roman war-god, from whom we get "martial" and "Martin," was to the Greeks Ares, god of vengeance. Ceres, goddess of the harvest, goes back to a root meaning "to grow or nurture," which also gives us "create" and "crescent." "Cereal" goes back directly to Ceres. Her Greek name was Demeter, from another root meaning "earth" or "soil," from which we also get "humus" and "human." The sea-god Neptune has his root in a word that means "cloud," and gives us "nebula" and "nebulose." The sun-god Apollo means "strength," while Cupid, god of love and desire, has his root in a word that means "to smoke or cook," which also gives us "vapor." The name of Venus, Roman goddess of beauty, comes from a root meaning "strive" or "love," from which we also get "venerate," "venison" and "wish."

Then there was Janus, god of doorways, who had two faces, since he had to look in two opposite directions at once. After him was named January, the first month of the year, which looks forward into the new year and backward into the old. Here the root word means "to go," and actually gives us "year," while Janus himself gives rise to such words as "janitor," a keeper of the *janua* or door.

Maia, wife of Vulcan, the fire-god, and mother of Mercury, the god of trade and travel, gave her name to the month of May, as well as to girls named May or Mae; her root word means "big" ("the big, old mother"), and it appears in a long series of words that include "mayor," "maximum," "majesty," "much," the *magni-* of "magnificent," the *mega-* of "megatron," and the *maha-* of "mahatma." Vesta, goddess of the hearth (her Greek name was Hestia, and her eternal fire was kept alive by the vestal virgins), takes her name from a root meaning "to dwell," which also gives us "was."

In addition to the major characters of the mythological world created by the Greeks and Romans, there were numerous other personages, some of them presiding over individual natural forces, such as Aeolus, god of the winds, who had under his command the specific winds, like Eurus and Zephyr (the latter's name still survives in the sense of a "soft, gentle breeze"). There were minor gods and goddesses who went in groups, like the Muses, whose name survives in "music," though music was only one of the arts and sciences over which they exercised their supervision. A few names of the individual Muses still appear in proper names, notably Clio, Thalia and Urania. There were the Dryads, tree goddesses (in fact, their name is from the same root that gives us "tree," as well as "Druids," the Celtic pagan priests of the tree-worship). There were the Nereids, or water-nymphs, who assisted Nereus, one of the sea-gods. One of the Nereids, Thetis, was the mother of Achilles, the Greek warrior in the Trojan War whose heel alone was vulnerable.

In addition to these rather pleasant characters, there were highly unpleasant ones, like the Furies and the Harpies, whose mission it was to persecute those who had displeased the gods. The name of the Furies goes back to a root that means "rain" or "mist," and that appears also in "February." That of the Harpies is connected with a "snatching up" root that we get also in "rapacious" and "ravish." Nemesis was the goddess of divine vengeance, and we still speak today of someone's nemesis. The Gorgons, whose name means "horrible ghost," were women with snakes in the place of hair; and whoever looked upon them was turned into stone. The Cyclops was the one-eyed giant who almost finished off Ulysses and his companions; his name means "round-eyed," and the *cycl-* part appears in "bicycle," while the *-ops* part is the same word that appears in "optical" and "optician."

Fabulous monsters were numerous: the Hydra, the Chimera (a monstrous goat, whose name goes back to a root that means "winter" or "snow," and which has given rise to the adjective "chimerical," or imaginary). Argus was the monster with a hundred eyes, while Cerberus was the three-headed dog who guarded the access into Hades, and a gruff gatekeeper or janitor is still occasionally referred to as a Cerberus. Scylla and Charybdis were the twin monsters who guarded the Strait of Messina, through which Ulysses had to pass in his travels, and the Italian equivalent for "between the devil and the deep sea" is still "between Scylla and Charybdis." Draco, who gives us "dragon" and "Dracula," was another mythical monster. Lares and Penates were the Roman household gods, and they are still occasionally spoken of in connection with household belongings.

The ancient Germanic tribes had an Olympus of their own called Valhalla, with gods and goddesses who more or less coincided with those of the Greeks and Romans, but bore entirely different names. Thor and Odin are the best known, but there was also Freya, goddess of love and beauty (like the Roman Venus and the Greek Aphrodite), whose name appears today in the form of Frieda. There was Loki the destroyer, god of mischief, whose root means, as you might expect, "to break," and appears also in "lugubrious." There were the Norns, corresponding to the Roman Fates, whose root word means "growl" or "snarl," and appears today in "snarl," "snore" and "snorkel." The Valkyrie, warrior-maidens of Valhalla, take their name from a root meaning "rip" or "rob," which also gives us "vulnerable." The Aesir was the collective name for the Teutonic Olympus, and they even had a collection of monsters and dragons, one of

whom, Grendel, appears in the earliest English work of
literature, the Anglo-Saxon "Beowulf."

Similar names appear in the mythology and religions
of the other peoples of antiquity. The Babylonians, Assy-
rians and Carthaginians had their Baal, Ishtar and
Moloch, the Egyptians their Amun-Ra, Isis and Osiris,
the Persians their Ormazd or Ahura-Mazda, and Ahriman
or Angra-Manyu, respectively the gods of good and evil
(the first part of Ahura-Mazda comes from the same root
as the Scandinavian Aesir, the second part from the same
root as the Greek Muses, showing the link among all
these ancient languages and religions). Mithra was a
later Persian god of light and friendship; his name comes
from a root that means "to bind," and gives rise to the
name of a Persian ruler, Mithridates. The Hindus had
and have their Brahma, Vishnu and Siva, along with
Indra, whose name appears also in the river Indus.

CHAPTER FIVE

The Names of The Classical World

The ancient world had numerous personages who bordered on the mythical, along with a wealth of historical characters whose names survive today.

The legend of Pygmalion and Galatea is still with us, now in the modern dress of *My Fair Lady*. Pygmalion, king of Cyprus, had made an ivory statue of a maiden, then proceeded to fall in love with the statue. In answer to his prayers, Aphrodite, goddess of love, gave the statue life, and they lived happily ever after (so the legend runs). Galatea's name came from a root meaning "bright" or "shining," and is related to our word "clean," while Pygmalion's name goes back to a word meaning "fist" or "fist-high," and is related to "Pygmy," "pug" and "puncture." Then there is the story of Daedalus, the first man to invent wings and fly, whose name means "cunning worker," being derived from a root that means "to split or hew." There is Prometheus, who stole fire from heaven and gave it to man. His name means "fore-thinker," and is related to "Muse," "music," "mood," "morose," "mathematics," and "Mazda," the Persian god of good. Nestor and Mentor, two wise counselors of the Greeks in the Trojan War, bear names which mean, respectively, "the one who always comes home" and "the thinker." Mentor is connected with "monitor," "mind," "memory," "mental," "monument," and the -*matic* suffix of "mathematics"; the word is still used today in the sense of "a teacher."

The name of Homer, the poet of the Trojan War and the wanderings of Ulysses, comes from a word that means "join, fit, ordain," and is claimed to mean specifically "the accompanier," or "the blind man who goes with one who leads him" (Homer was reputed to be blind). The same root appears in the *Arta-* of Artaxerxes, the great Persian emperor, but with the meaning of "law" or "holy right." Phaedrus was a name borne both by a Greek philosopher and a Roman writer of fables. Its root means "bright."

In the historical, as distinguished from the mythological, world of the ancient Greeks, there were many names that have become highly famous: Thucydides, Euripides, Plato, Aristotle, Sophocles, Aristophanes. These names are still in current use among the modern Greeks. Without going into them at too great length, it may be well to remember that the Greek word for "wisdom" appears in the *Soph-* of Sophocles, as well as in Sofia or Sophia; that the *Aristo-* of names like Aristophanes and Aristides means "best"; that the *Andro-* of Androcles is "man"; and the *Alex-* of Alexander and Alexis is "defense." Eleutherius means "free," and the name was recently borne by one of the great modern Greek statesmen, Eleutherius Venizelos. Two very common Greek names that have great currency among us today are Agatha, "good," and Margaret, "pearl."

Roman names are even more current today. Fulvius, Flavius and Flavia go back to a root that means "light-colored," and are good examples of descriptive names. Fabius, which gives rise to our Fabian, has its roots in a word meaning "bean"; Fabius Maximus, surnamed Cunctator, or "delayer," was the Roman general who finally wore out the Carthaginian Hannibal by his delaying tactics, and a Fabian Socialist today is one who wishes to reach the Socialist goal by a policy of gradualness. Augustus comes from a word that means "to increase." Justus and Justinian have the root of "just" and "justice," Clement and Clementine have that of "mercy," Constance and Constantine that of "steadfastness," Valerius, Valerian, Valeria and Valentine that of "valor," Flora and Florence that of "flower." Vincent is a "winner." Clara means "bright," and is the exact Latin translation of the Germanic Bertha, while the masculine Clarence could be used as the equivalent of Bert. Beatrix or Beatrice is the "one who gives happiness." Silvester is the "forest-dweller." Mark, Marcus, Martial, Martin, Marius and the very common Spanish and Italian Mario all go back to Mars, god of war. The names of Roman emperors are often highly descriptive. Septimius Severus, for instance, combines the word for "seventh" with that for "stern" or "severe."

The Romans, in their constant wars with the Gauls and Britons, brought back a certain number of Celtic names. A very common name suffix among the Gaulish chieftains was -*rix*, which is precisely the same word as the Latin *rex*, meaning "king" (the same word appears in the Germanic -*reich* or -*ric*, the English "right," "rich" and "rule," even in India's *rajah*). Two Gaulish chiefs mentioned by Caesar in his Gallic Wars are Dumnorix and Vercingetorix. From Britain the Romans brought back the name of Queen Boadicea, who resisted their power to the end. Her name is more properly rendered as Boudicca, and goes back to a root that means "rich in victory"; the name, unfortunately for her, was not prophetic, since it was the Romans who won.

CHAPTER SIX

Biblical and Religious Names

The Old Testament, as we have seen, provides a never-ending source of Hebrew and Aramaic names, of which a great many are in common use today.

Practically every name that ends in -*el* is of Hebrew origin (the -*el* suffix is Hebrew for "God" or "of God"). The names of the Archangels Michael and Gabriel mean, respectively, "he who is like God" and "man of God." Raphael is "God hath healed," Daniel is "God is my judge," Manuel or Emmanuel is "God is with us," Gamaliel is "God's reward," and Joel is "the Lord is God." The *el* appears as a prefix in Elizabeth, "consecrated to God," and in Elihu, "the Lord is Jehovah," as well as in many other names. Had we no other knowledge of the Hebrews, this list of names alone would be mighty testimony to the fact that they were, and are, a religious, God-fearing people, dedicated to spiritual achievement.

The name of Jehovah or Jahweh appears in disguised form, as required by Hebrew custom, in such names as Zachary or Zachariah ("Jehovah hath remembered"), Uriah ("flame of Jehovah"), Matthew ("gift of Jehovah"), Jeremiah ("exalted of Jehovah"). Ezra is "help." Simon (or Simeon) means "granted by God in answer to a prayer." Joseph means "will increase."

Joseph and John are among the most common names in use today. The Hebrew form of John is Yōhānān, "Jahweh hath been gracious." Its popularity is attested by the list in the calendar of Christian saints of no fewer than one hundred Saint Johns, with John the Baptist and John the Evangelist heading the list. It is also indicative of the name's vogue that it spreads, in one form or another, often as a diminutive, to a variety of persons and things. John Bull is the symbol of Britain; John Doe and its feminine form, Jane Doe, are used in legal documents when the person's name is unknown. There was a "Dear John" form of letter that achieved some notoriety during World War II. Putting your "John Hancock" on a letter means signing it legibly (when the Declaration of Independence was signed, John Hancock stated that he would write his name so large that George III would be able to read it without spectacles). We have an "Honest John" guided missile. Johnny Reb was the nickname of the Confederate soldier (at least to the Yankees) in our Civil War. Johnny-come-lately, Johnny-on-the-spot, Stage-door Johnny, are terms in common use. We even have Jack-of-all-trades and, in fable, Jack-the-Giant-Killer.

Christianity, beginning with Christ Himself, gives us a long list of Christian names. Jesus is not a common name among English speakers, but the Spanish-speaking world makes constant use of it as a first name. On the other hand, we have Christian, Christina (with Kirsten as a Scandinavian variant), Christopher, or "Christ bearer" (St. Christopher carried a child across a swollen stream not knowing that the child was Christ; the information came to him when he arrived exhausted, but with his burden safe, on the other bank). The name Christ itself is not Hebrew, but Greek; the Hebrew form is Messiah. Both words mean "anointed," and we find the root of the Greek word not only in Christ, but also in "chrism," "cream," "grime" and "grist." Jesus, on the other hand, is the Hebrew Joshua, and means "God is deliverance."

Greek Christian names are numerous. Baptiste, a very popular French name, means "he who baptizes," and Anastasia is "pertaining to the Resurrection." "Gifts of the Lord" in Greek range from Theodore and Theodora or Theodosia to Dorothea, Dorothy and plain Dora (the *theo-* part of the name means "God," the *-dore* or *-dora* portion is "gift").

Latin supplies us with Dominic, "pertaining to the Lord" (*Dominus*), which has relatives in the Romance words for "Sunday," "the day of the Lord": *dimanche* in French, *domingo* in Spanish, *domenica* in Italian. Noël, sometimes anglicized into Newell, is *Natalis*, "pertaining to the birth (of Christ)"; it also is the French word for Christmas. Benedict is "blessed" and Pius is "devoted." It is only fair to state, however, that the name Pius was in use when the Romans were still pagans.

The custom of bestowing names of saints upon an individual, thus calling upon the saint to be his patron or protector and endow him with the saint's own virtues, arose about the tenth century. Today many Christian churches frown upon the practice of bestowing any name except one that appears in the Bible or in the list of saints. Fortunately, both sources are so vast that there is an almost infinite range of choice. Most of the old pagan names, Greek, Latin, Germanic, Celtic, or others from even earlier civilizations, were at one time or another in the early Middle Ages borne by a person who later became a saint. In this way, many names of pagan origin and connotation have been, so to speak, naturalized into the Church and made thoroughly fit for Christian use. Not only individuals, but cities, regions and entire countries have their patron saints. Saint George (the name was originally Greek, and meant "farmer") is the patron of the city of Genoa, of the region of Catalonia in Spain, and of England, Russia and Portugal. Saint Nicholas (this Greek name originally meant "conquering host") not only turns into our Santa Claus, but is the patron saint of the city of Bari in southern Italy, and of Greece. Saint Denis, Saint Genevieve, Saint Germaine, are among the patrons of France and of French cities. Saint Mark protects Venice, and Saint Ambrose protects Milan. Saint Patrick, though the name is Roman in origin, is the great patron saint of Ireland; Saint David takes care of Wales, and Saint Andrew of Scotland.

The practice of calling upon saints for help and protection gives rise to curious misconceptions. In France, Saint Vincent is often prayed to by wine growers because the first syllable of his name coincides with the French word for "wine," *vin*. Saint Ouen (to us he would be

Owen) receives the pleas of the deaf because of erroneous connection of his name with the verb *ouir*, "to hear." Saint Michael the Archangel occasionally intercedes for bakers because of the fact that the French word for "loaf" is *miche*. Saint Expédit expedites matters. In German-speaking lands, Saint Lambert is prayed to by the lame (the German *lahm*, "lame," sounds like the beginning of the name), and Saint Gallus by those who suffer with their gall-bladders.

Spain and Italy have typical Christian feminine names, which coincide with forms of Catholic belief. Concepción in Spanish, Concetta in Italian, remind their owners of the Immaculate Conception. The Italian Rosario and Rosaria are the rosary, and Annunziata, often incorrectly rendered in English as Nancy, is a reminder of the Annunciation; the Spanish Mercedes is the "mercies of God," Consuelo is "consolation," Dolores is "sorrows" (of the Virgin). The Spanish Carmen, feminine, and the Italian Carmine (masculine) and Carmela (feminine), refer to Our Lady of Mount Carmel.

Protestant countries have similar practices, as evidenced by several English and Puritan names still in vogue today (Prudence, Faith, Hope, Charity, Piety, even Justice, Silence and True Love). Under Oliver Cromwell, when the Puritans ruled England, some rather complicated names made their appearance, like that of Unless-Christ-had-died-for-thee-thou-hadst-been-damned Barebones, the authentic name of the founder of England's first fire insurance company. His father, incidentally, a political figure who gave his name to the

Barebones Parliament of 1653, was Praise-God Barebones.

Germanic names that extol God are relatively few, as against the many we have seen that extol prowess in warfare and leadership. Still, we have Godfrey (or Gottfried, in its German version, or Geoffrey, Jeffrey in the later French development), which means "God's peace," along with Godwin, "God's friend" and Goddard, "God's strength." The *Os-* of Oscar, Oswald, Osmond, is also a reference to God.

Religious names abound in countries whose faith does not stem from the Old or New Testaments. Krishna Menon, India's ambassador to the United Nations, bears the name of a Hindu god. Abdullah is Arabic for "servant of Allah," or God, and Abd-el-Nasser, President of the Arab Republic which includes Egypt and Syria, means "the servant of the victorious one" (Nasser, "the victorious," is one of the many Arabic designations for God). Buddha, the religious name of Gautama, founder of the Buddhist faith, comes from a root that means "to be awake or enlightened."

By way of contrast, the devil ("devil" comes from a Greek word meaning "slanderer," "traducer") bears three chief names, of which one, Satan, is Hebrew, and means "adversary." Another, Mephistopheles, is Greek (it seems to have no particular meaning, but was first applied in the Middle Ages). The third, Lucifer, is Latin, and means "light-bearer"; it was the name of the chief archangel before his revolt against God and his fall into the depths of the inferno.

CHAPTER SEVEN

Names of the English-Speaking World

If one picks up a book like *The Golden Warrior*, in which long lists of Anglo-Saxon names appear, he is struck by the vast continuing change in naming practices since the days that preceded the Norman Conquest. The names of the Anglo-Saxons included many Alfgars, Leofgars, Ansgars and Edgars (the *-gar* suffix means "spear," and only Edgar survives in common use today); many Ethelreds, Ethelwolds, Ethelrics and Athelstanes (*Ethel-* or *Athel-* is "noble"; Ethel survives in general use); many Alfreds, Elfgivas and Elfridas (*Alf-* or *Elf-* is "elf," and Alfred and Elfrida are still with us); many Wulfstans, Wulfnoths and Wulfwins, along with Godwin, Frewin, Leofwin (*Wulf-* is "wolf," *-win* is "friend"; the former does not survive very well, the latter does); a multitude of *Eds* ("property or wealth"; most of these are still here); and a scattering of Brihtwolds ("bright

48

forest"), Cuthberts ("noted splendor," and still with us),
Leofrics, Aldiths and Godivas. The Anglo-Saxons were
Christians by the time the Normans arrived, but the
practice of naming people after saints had not yet gotten
under way, and the old Germanic names were still in
full swing. The French-speaking Normans introduced
Germanic names from the Frankish and Scandinavian
branches, along with numerous Greek and Latin names
they had acquired, and most of the old Anglo-Saxon
names not borne by a saint quietly disappeared from the
scene.

It has been estimated that in the twelfth century, immediately after the Norman Conquest, 38 per cent of
recorded men's names consisted of Henry, John, Robert,
William and Richard. By the fourteenth century, these
five names alone accounted for 64 per cent of the total,
a clear indication of a shift in vogue.

Protestantism introduced a larger proportion of Old
Testament names than had been in use formerly. It was
left to the Puritans to exercise their imagination in a
God-fearing way, with the result that we have such combinations as Sorry-for-sin and Through-much-tribulation-
we-enter-the-kingdom-of-heaven. These names spread to
America, and we have a record of a Whom-the-Lord-
Preserved Scott whom his friends fondly called "Canned"
Scott. In one locality in Nebraska (Filley) a researcher
found such names as Quo Vadis Marie McGinnis and
Eccehomo Thrapp, which seem to hark back to the early
days of Christianity. He also found Naughty-Bird Kirk-
sey and Spengler Arlington Brough, but these can hardly
be blamed on the Puritans. American ingenuity in piling

up first names to an extent that might be envied by a prince of a ruling house of Europe appears in the records of an Ohio draft board, with Noah Harvey Herman Daniel Boone Buster Brown David Longworth. Luckily, there are not too many such formations, and the Puritan names seem to be dying out.

A couple of Anglo-American practices in the matter of feminine names are worth noting. One is the use of certain names of months (April, May, June) as first names for girls. The only name of a fall or winter month reported is January, masculine, and the summer months, July and August, are applied to both genders (Jules, Julius, Julia, Julian; Augustus, Augusta). The other is the multiplication of variant forms of feminine names, either in spelling, or in pronunciation, or both. Bridget, Bridgette, Brydget, is a mild case. The feminine form of John leads us from Jane, Jean, Jeanne and Joan on to Janet, Jeannette, Janice, Joanne, Joanna, Johanna, and others.

Two practices that occasionally bewilder foreigners are our Senior, Junior, and even Third and Fourth appended to a name (for this, though, there is a precedent in Roman practice, with Cato and Pliny appearing in Elder and Younger variants), and the practice of using family names as first names. The latter is prima-facie evidence of Protestantism, since the Catholic Church would frown upon a first name that was not of Biblical or religious origin (note, however, the first name of Bishop Fulton Sheen, indicating that the prohibition may be relaxed on occasion).

A partial list of family names that are currently and widely used as first names includes Ashley, Warren, Wallace, Stanley, Willard, Sinclair, Seymour, Nelson, Lloyd, Clayton, Clifford, Lawton and Parker. In the feminine division we find Lynn, Leslie, Beverly and Shirley, but these names, in certain parts of the country, are ambivalent, being indifferently handed out to men or women, which further baffles the foreigner in our midst. Other ambisexual names in the English-speaking world are Merle, Evelyn, Marion, Vivian, and, in spoken form, Francis-Frances.

Many studies have been made of first-name popularity in America, but they are generally inconclusive, because the picture is forever changing with the times, with hitherto unheard-of names suddenly becoming popular by reason of some historical event (Kim, for example, came into vogue at the time of the Korean war; it was originally a Korean name).

One such study informs us that we have over four million Marys and six million Johns, and that Mary is followed in popularity by Elizabeth, Barbara, Dorothy, Helen and Margaret, in that order, while John has as its competitors William, Charles, James, George and Robert. A Gallup poll confirms the figures for John, but states that within the past ten years Linda has crowded all the feminine contestants, including even Mary, out of the picture. Its complete breakdown for names bestowed between 1946 and 1956 runs as follows: Linda, Mary, Deborah, Susan, Carol, Patricia, Catherine, Margaret, Barbara, Karen, on the distaff side; for males, John, Michael, James, Robert, William, David, Thomas, Stephen, Richard, Joseph. Names crowded out of the picture since 1906 include Ruth, Anne, Helen, Ellen,

Dorothy, Elizabeth and Frances, along with George, Charles, Frank, Albert and Louis. Temporary vogue during the years between 1916 and 1946 was achieved by Mildred, Edith, Shirley, Judith, Joan, and by Clarence, Edward and Ronald. High on the list for the last decade, though not among the first ten, are Sharon, Nancy, Carolyn and Janice, along with Gary, Ronald, Loren and Gerald.

There is also a study of first and second name combinations, in which the six most frequent are: Fred Smith, Charles Johnson, Henry Brown, William Jones, Robert Wilson and John Anderson. This brings into the picture one first name that seems to have no great vogue all by itself, namely Fred or Frederick, an old Germanic name that means "rich in peace."

CHAPTER EIGHT

Names of Endearment (And Otherwise)

It is fairly evident by now that a good many of our more picturesque descriptive first names began their careers as nicknames, whether pleasing or not to their recipients. There is absolutely nothing new about the nickname in its etymological sense (an eke-name, or an additional name). In antiquity, Sophocles was surnamed the Bee, and Chrysostom the Light, one on account of his activity, the second because of his enlightenment of others. This is highly reminiscent of such current nicknames as the Body, the Voice, the Fingers, and even underworld forms like Scarface or Greasy Thumb. To his friends, Disraeli, the great British statesman, was Dizzy, and John Keats's name was telescoped into Junkets.

It was the Romans who dignified what was in origin a nickname to the point where it became an accepted part of a person's full identity. In the name of Marcus Tullius

53

Cicero, the first name is a personal name, the second indicates that he belonged to the Tullian clan, and might be described as a family name. The third, which, as we have seen, means "chick-pea," and came from a wart on the nose of one of his ancestors, later became traditional in the family. In like manner we have Caius (or Gaius) Julius Caesar, the last name coming from the root of a verb meaning "to cut," and indicating that somewhere along the line there had been what even today goes by the name of a Caesarian birth. Quintus Horatius Flaccus, better known to American students of Latin as Horace, had a third name that originally meant "flabby" or "flap-eared." Publius Ovidius Naso (Ovid) had a third name that meant "nose" or "long-nosed," and Publius Virgilius Maro (Virgil) bore a last name that was the designation of an Etruscan magistrate (Virgil came from northern Italy, where the people of Etruscan stock were numerous, and it is not at all surprising that one of his ancestors should have been a magistrate).

Today, certain business organizations (Rotary, Lions, Kiwanis, etc.) encourage good fellowship by requiring members to be first-named or, preferably, nicknamed at social meetings. We even have nickname clubs, which make a practice of endowing their members with the proper "handles." One organization of younger people, located in New York's Mulberry Street section, has a membership list which includes Big Joe Red, Louie Bugs, the Trieste Kid, Johnny Pepper Repper Depper, the Skull, Baby Ralph the Horse, Danny Feet, Wheaties, Duke Zwick, Jiminy Crickets, Little Wolf, Spy, Spoon Head, Louie Beans, Bobbie Grandma, Brother Beaver,

Tonsils, Peppy Bobalu, Sandy Hop, Billy Meow, Lefty Al the G. I. Pal, Dangerous Dan McGoon, Tommy La La, Jackie Fish Hole and, in its feminine auxiliary, Mary Findo Twee-Twee. It is to be emphasized that the bearers of these names are not at all juvenile delinquents, but simply young people who like to exercise their fervid Italian imagination. It will also be noted that in many cases the naming process differs not at all from the one we have seen operating for the American Indians or the early Germanic tribes.

There is another type of nickname which involves a lengthening or shortening of a legitimate first name. In this class we find the Ike occasionally applied by the space-saving headlines to President Eisenhower, and the Cal bestowed on one of his predecessors in office, Calvin Coolidge. We also find abbreviations consisting of initials, as in the case of F.D.R. for Franklin Delano Roosevelt. Mac is often used for a person whose name begins with Mac or Mc, or as a general form of address for a man whose name one does not know, but this is a somewhat vulgar practice.

Name lengthening is not too frequent in the Anglo-Saxon world, which prefers monosyllabic forms, but in countries given to resonant polysyllables you find additions such as Giorgione, "Big George," and Masaccio, "Bad Tom" (Giorgione and Masaccio were two famous Italian Renaissance painters). But Masaccio, although it has the pejorative suffix -accio, which gives the meaning of "bad" to whatever name it is added to, is a cut-down form of Tommasaccio. Italian also shows such abbreviated forms as Dino for an Aldobrandino of Germanic origin which means "Little old sword"; only the last consonant of the original name and the diminutive suffix *-ino* remain.

The English-speaking world specializes in short forms, like Ned and Ted, more or less interchangeably used for Edward and Theodore, or Peggy for Margaret, Mandy for Amanda (a Latin name that means "lovable"), and Mamie, also claimed to be a short form of Margaret, though there is a possibility that it may represent Old French *m'amie*, "my (girl) friend."

The evolution of Margaret into Peggy is interesting. The steps in between are Marge, Mag, Meg, Peg, Peggy. There are also Margery, Marjorie and Margot. In German, the equivalent of Margaret (Margareta) goes into such forms as Greta, Grete and Gretchen, while Charlotte becomes Lotta and Lotte (like the English Lottie). Dorothy lends itself to Dottie and Dot, Gertrude to either Gertie or Trudie, Mary to Molly, Polly to Minnie. Elizabeth runs the gamut of Eliza, Lisa, Lizzie and Libby on the one hand, of Betty, Betsy, Bess, Beth and Babette on the other. Ann goes to Nan, Nancy and Nanette, along with the obvious Annie and the Spanish Anita. Wilhelmina gives rise to Mina, Sarah to Sally, Penelope to Penny, Dolores to Lola, Louise to Lulu. There is Sue from Susan, Cindy from Lucinda, Nellie from Eleanor, Tilly from Matilda, Trixie from Beatrix. Bridgit has Bridie and Biddy as its favorite diminutives, and from Catherine we get Kate, Kitty and Kay.

Masculine names, too, lend themselves to abbreviated forms; Tony, Joe, Jim, Fred, Hank for Harry (Henry), Barney (from either Barnabas or Bernard), Kit (from

Christopher). One we don't hear often in this country is Hodge from Roger. Jack is used as the diminutive of John, but actually comes from the French Jacques, which is James. Austin or Austen is a shortening of Augustine.

Countries speaking languages other than English use affectionate diminutives to the same extent that we do. The Russians use Misha as a diminutive of Michael, Sasha for Sergei, Sonya for Sofia, Tanya for Tatiana. The German Hans and Fritz (from Johannes and Friedrich) have been popularized by the comic strips. French diminutive forms often end in -on, which would give you an augmentative (that is, a word that means "big" instead of "little") in Spanish or Italian: Madelon is "little Madeleine," and Marion is little Mary, or Molly. The favorite Spanish diminutive endings are -ita and -ito (Pepita for Josefa, Manuelito for Manuel). Italian has -ino and -ina (Franceschino, Giovannina), but also an entire series of other cut-down forms, like Beppe for Joe, Rigo for Arrigo (Harry), Tilde for Matilde.

It is of interest to note how diminutive forms often get into stock expressions or clichés, just like regular names ("doubting Thomas," "Dumb Dora," "Simple Simon"). We have all heard of Tom, Dick and Harry, of G. I. Joe, of the George whom you are supposed to let do it, of a good-time Charlie. Smart Aleck (from Alexander) was recently defined by the Speaker of the British House of Commons as "not derogatory or opprobrious" when applied by an M. P. (Member of Parliament) to an opposition member. Skeezix is an altogether imaginary nickname.

One final note about terms of endearment (though

these are not, properly speaking, proper names) comes up in a poll taken to determine the most popular salutations given by husbands to their wives. The winners, in order named: Dear, Darling, Baby, Honey, Sweetheart, Dearest, Precious.

CHAPTER NINE

Personal Name Oddities

It has often been remarked by foreigners that Americans are much given to bestowing combination names, which generally unite into a single form the names of both parents, or of two favorite grandparents. That we are not the only ones to indulge in this practice is shown by such German forms as Marlene (a contraction of Maria Magdalene), or the originally French Marianne (Marie plus Anne; in fact. Marianne even represents France in the same fashion that John Bull typifies England and Uncle Sam the United States).

There is, however, little doubt that Americans are addicted to this custom to a greater degree than other peoples. It is easy in our country to find such combination names as Georgianna (George plus Anna), Joanna (often meant to represent precisely Joe plus Anna, rather than to function as one of the feminine forms of John),

Charlene (Charles plus Lena). We can even find Lugene (Louise and Eugene), Johnina (John and Nina), Adnelle (Addison and Nellie) and Marmina (Margaret and Wilhelmina). One of the best samples we have found combines the initial syllables of the names of four grandparents, who were named Elkanah, Daniel, Rebecca and Mary; what came out was Eldarema, which nobody can deny is a somewhat unusual name.

But Americans do more. When the existing roster does not supply them with a name they deem sufficiently picturesque, they do not hesitate to coin one for their children. In this fashion we have had reported to us Zania, Opiot, Maya, Joslena, Cricelda, Aasine, Erbutus, Capitola, Esina, Letha, Nudine and Palestrube on the feminine side; and on the masculine, Nylon, Clave, Eenos, Ewel, Jetro and Rearis.

It cannot be squarely asserted that this characteristic is American alone. The British Government, through the mouth of the Commonwealth Relations Secretary, ruled some time ago that registrars have no right to interfere when parents choose a name for a child unless the name is distinctly objectionable. "Not Wanted" was the name that brought on the decision. Such names as Postscript, Caboose and Seaborn appear on both sides of the ocean. No Britisher, however, has been known to receive the name of States' Rights, which is not unknown in our South.

Poland recently passed a law permitting people to get rid of names which are "ludicrous and humiliating," and thus to obtain a fresh start in life. Among the names that brought on the law were such gems as Kielbasa, "Sausage," and Piwko, "Small Beer," along with other forms like "Big Ox" or "Little Drum." It seems that in eighteenth-century Poland, when family names for poorer persons were coming into fashion, feudal landlords took delight in giving peasants names that the landlords regarded as funny. The laughing, if any, goes the other way now.

Another quaint custom (this, too, appears elsewhere, notably in royal and noble European families) is that of bestowing a long series of names. We have already seen a fairly long one from Ohio, but the best one reported comes from Liverpool, England. In 1880, an unfortunate child whose family name was Pepper received the following set of handles: Anna Bertha Cecilia Diana Emily Fanny Gertrude Hypatia Inez Jane Kate Louise Maud Nora Ophelia Quince Rebecca Starkey Teresa Ulysis Venus Winifred Xenophone Yetty Zeno, with every letter of the alphabet represented, and only a couple of improbable forms in evidence. Not to be outdone, the United States more recently graduated from the Pellston, Mich., High School a girl whose name was Aleatha Beverly Carol Diana Eva Felice Greta Harline Io Joanne Karen Laquita Maurine Naomi Orpha Patricia Queenie Rebecca Shirley Teresa Una Valeeta Wanda Xelia Yolanda Zoe Kalkofen. For the record, the English girl went through life with the single name of Annie, and the American requested the reporters to "just call her Pat."

Variants of these fads are fairly numerous. One appears when the parents insist that all their children should have names beginning with a single letter of the alphabet. This leads, in the family of a well-known rock-and-roller, to the series Antoinette, Antoine III, Andre, Anatole, Anola and Andrea. But Europe betters this feat with a Parisian music teacher whose eight children bore the names Doh, Ray, Me, Fah, Sol, La, Ti and Octave.

CHAPTER TEN

Translatable and Untranslatable Names

Foreigners are often left wondering and breathless when confronted with some of our imaginative first names. We, too, are very often baffled by some of the foreign names that we encounter.

It is not only those names for which there is no possible translation into another tongue. It is even the old, familiar names that can assume very unfamiliar forms.

For instance, the familiar Greek name Alexander ("defender of men") has a Scottish form, Alastair or Alistair, but very few people identify the Scottish with the English name. Inez is the Spanish version of Agnes; both names are current with us, and few people realize that it is the same name. Herman is "army man" in Germanic form; Armand is the very same name in French form. Another Germanic name is Alberic, "elf ruler"; who would identify it with Aubrey, which is the form it takes in French? It is the same with Theodoric and Diedrich, Thierry and Terry, with Maurice and Morris, with Nicholas and Colin, even with Benedict and Bennett.

Some names, those of very well-known Biblical personages and saints in particular, are quite international, and usually easy to recognize. John would probably be recognized under the form of Jean (French), Juan (Spanish), João (Portuguese), Giovanni (Italian), Johannes (German), Jens (Danish), Ian (Scottish), Jan (Polish), Ivan (Russian), Jovan (Serbian); but the Irish Sean, the Finnish Juhana, the Hungarian János might give trouble. James runs the gamut of Jacques (French), Diego or Jaime (Spanish), Giacomo (Italian). Frank or Francis can be François (French), Francisco (Spanish), Francesco (Italian), Franz (German), then go on to Ferencz in Hungarian and František in Czech. Joseph is José in Spanish, Jozef in Polish, Josip in Serbian, Yusuf in Arabic. Pavel is Russian, and Povel Danish for Paul. George takes the form of Jerzi in Polish and Jiři in Czech.

We could even play a guessing game with some names. Here is one which is Pyotr in Russian, Peder in Danish, Pietari in Finnish: what is it in English? That was rather easy. Here is a tougher one: French Etienne, Irish Stiobhan, Spanish Esteban, Hungarian István; or Italian Luigi, Norwegian Ludvig, Hungarian Lájos.

In Russian, the names that in English have *th* will appear, when they do, with an *f*. What are the English equivalents of the Russian Fedor, Timofei and Marfa? You can figure out the French Guillaume, the Spanish Guillermo, the Italian Guglielmo easily enough by remembering that a Germanic *w* comes into the Romance languages, usually, as *gu*. If you want to try yourself out still further, here is a supplementary list: Polish Wincenty, Tadeusz, Szymon; Scandinavian Edvard, Anders, Harald; Serbian Danilo, Mirko, Gyorgye; Hungarian Sándor, Ilona, Bálint (the last is really unfair; the names are Alexander, Helen, Valentine).

So far, we have been able to translate them, though with a little trouble. But we must not forget that every language has a series of names which have no translation, save perhaps into a language of a kindred family. These are normally left untranslated, just like a family name. Polish has a long list, which includes Kazimir, Bolesłaus, Bronisław, Jadwiga, Wacław, Żegota. In the Scandinavian tongues we find Olaf, Niels, Sören, Gunno, Haakon, Hjalmar, Halfdan. Russian has Boris, Igor, Tatiana, Vladimir, Vissarion, Taras. Serbian has Stojan, Milan, Dushan, Vuk, Sima, Draga and Ljuba. Finnish gives us Peutti, Kauppis, Heikki, Arwid, Alkio. Hungarian has Árpád, Béla, Géza, Tihamér, Zsolt. There is no translating the Italian Alfio, the French Gaston, the Spanish Eloy, the Czech Jaroslav.

Away from the familiar languages of Europe, we find that the Arabic Ali and Hassan, the Turkish Murad and Selim, the Persian Sohrab and Omar have to be left as they are (though we have turned the name of the founder of a great Persian religion, Zarathustra, into Zoroaster).

Of course, we must not give up too easily when we attempt to translate. It took us some time and effort to discover that the Hungarian Imre is the German Emmerich, which also becomes the Italian Amerigo, and ultimately leads to the name of America.

The question of how to pronounce untranslated names is a thorny one. The best advice is to do the best you can if you are not acquainted with the pronunciation of the language from which the name comes. As in the case of place names, there are guides to the pronunciation of foreign proper names for the use of radio announcers. It is an old trick for a language to assimilate to its own rules of pronunciation an untranslated foreign name. In this way we got Pansy from the French *pensée* ("thought"), Amy from the French *aimée* ("beloved"), Mabel from the French *ma belle* ("my lovely one"; though there is another theory that Mabel is a shortened form of Amabel, "lovable").

At the same time, there should not be too much distortion. In the radio advertising for a certain film, the name of the King of the Huns, also known as "the Scourge of God," Attila, with stress on the first syllable, was constantly mispronounced as at-TIL-lah; this may have been due to the influence of "gorilla," or of Godzilla, another monster, not in human form, that had gotten into pictures; at any rate, the final stage was reached when the newspaper advertising for the film misspelled the name in accordance with the new and incorrect pronunciation: "Atilla."

Do foreigners mishandle our names? Slightly. One reporter in Brazil informs us that he was a trifle puzzled by a reference to a play said to be by Shakespeare, and entitled "Omelette," until it dawned upon him that the name was "Hamlet." The Japanese pronunciation of Edgar Allen Poe is Edogowa Rampo.

In the matter of writing, when we transcribe Japanese

and Chinese names, we adapt them to our system of spelling. Other nations adapt them to theirs. The rather curious result is that a Japanese name which appears as Tosho in our transcription becomes Toscio in an Italian one, while our Machi-ko is their Macico. What happens to second names is a story that will be told a little later.

Part II

FAMILY NAMES

CHAPTER ELEVEN

How They Began

Personal names appear to have been among the earliest language forms used by man. By way of contrast, family names, at least in the form in which we know them, are latecomers. Yet their roots are to be found in antiquity, among peoples who, like the Hebrews, Greeks and Romans, had achieved a high level of civilization.

There is another curious fact about family names, or what might pass as such. After their early appearance in antiquity, they almost vanish during the early Middle Ages, to reappear in modern dress from the tenth century on.

The basic reason for second names is generally admitted to be the need to distinguish between two or more persons bearing the same first name. In an imaginary community in which there are several men all named John, it becomes almost imperative to make the

distinction. One easy way to do this is to call one John
the son of Peter, another John the son of William. A
second way is to distinguish between John who lives on
the hill and John who lives near the village well. Then
there is the possibility of distinguishing between John
the baker and John the tailor. Lastly, one John may have
a special physical or moral quality that distinguishes him;
his hair may be white, or he may be lame, or he may be
a very good person.

Right here we have our four basic family-name formations: the father's name, also called patronymic, resulting
in John Peterson (or John Peters, or John Pierson), John
Williamson (or Wilson, or Williams, or Wills); the location name (John Hillman, John Atwell); the professional
or trade name (John Baker, John Taylor); and the descriptive name (John White, John Cruikshanks, John
Good or Goodman).

These four methods of forming second or family names
do not by any means exhaust all the possibilities; but
they do constitute the major sources of our second names.

As in the case of place names and first names, we are
struck by the fact that these basic name-forming processes appear wherever the state of civilization is such as
to produce a double name. Languages and customs may
and do show wide variations; but the same or similar
forms, in different language attire, crop up again and
again, all over the globe. Even where one method is
favored to the practical exclusion of the others, it is im-
possible to classify that method as the property of one
particular race or group. The patronymic, or process
whereby one is identified by being described as the son

of another, was at one time used almost exclusively by
some Semitic groups, like the Hebrews and the Arabs;
but it was also used by the earliest Greek tribes and by
the ancient and modern Icelanders.

If we take such primitive groups as the American
Indians, we find that in their original state they favor
the single descriptive name, even though it consists in
English translation of two or more words (compare native
forms like Hiawatha, Minnehaha, Pocahontas, Powhatan,
Massassoit, Tecumseh, Osceola, Sequoia, with forms in
English translation, like Sitting Bull, Black Hawk, Thunder Cloud, Rain-in-the-Face). When the Indian acquires
the arts of western civilization, he may take on a Christian first name (like Geronimo), but even then he usually
retains as a second name the translated form of his original Indian name. In a present-day Crow tribe have been
found such names as Donald and Agnes Deernose,
Henry and Stella Old Coyote, Lloyd Little Hawk, Fred
Two Warriors, Tom and Susie Yellowtail, Henry Rides
the Horse. Two Iroquois names that appeared recently
in newspaper columns, Wallace Mad Bear Anderson and
Donald Falling Wind Richmond, show a tendency to
compromise with the white man's naming customs to the
extent of sandwiching the Indian name between an ordinary first and an equally commonplace last English name.

But the Indian naming process does not basically differ
from the white man's. Taking a list of American names
at random, we encounter, preceded by a first name, such
English family names as Duet, Forehand, French, O'Bear
and Shortliffe. French is a name indicating national
origin, and does not differ too much from Mohawk or

Chippewa. O'Bear is at the same time a patronymic, indicating descent, and a totem name, and could be compared to Old Coyote or Little Hawk. The other three are descriptive names indicating some characteristic or activity, and have their counterparts in Rides the Horse and Deernose.

In the white man's list, which is thoroughly American, we find several names of foreign origin, which, when analyzed, reveal the same mental processes at work. Here are the originally French Billetdoux, Lemieux, Letendre, Leveque and Larrabee. The first means "love note," the second is "the best," the third is "the tender one," the fourth is "the bishop," and the last comes from an original *l'Arabie* and means "Arabia." Best and Bishop translate perfectly as second names into English, indicating one a quality (as is also the case with Letendre), the other a profession. Billetdoux would seem to indicate a favorite activity of the bearer's ancestors, and Larrabee a country of origin. We also find three Italian names, Bongiorno, Linsalata and La Morte, meaning "good day," "the salad" and "death." The first might indicate a favorite form of greeting, the second a favorite food. The third could be variously explained as a professional name (undertakers among the bearer's ancestors) or a characteristic (an ancestor who was "death" to the foes he met in battle).

There could easily be errors in our interpretation, and there could be many other possibilities, but names of this sort will serve to indicate the general process of formation. It goes without saying that in the same list the Williamsons, Hills, Taylors, Smiths, Browns and

Goodmans are far more numerous than the names we have picked out for purposes of illustration.

In antiquity, it was the Romans who achieved the nearest approach to the naming system we have today, with a first or personal name, a clan name definitely passed on from father to son, and a nickname often becoming hereditary, so that Marcus Tullius Cicero would coincide rather closely in formation with Henry Wadsworth Longfellow. It is rather surprising that once the Romans had achieved this method their descendants should have discarded it after the fall of the Empire to return to the single name that seems indicative of a lower level of civilization; but almost at once the new process which gives us the naming system of today began to appear, with early writers distinguished, as they had often been even in classical times, by their place of birth (Gregory of Tours, Francis of Assisi), or by a descriptive characteristic (Lambert le Tort, "Lambert the Twisted," the name of an Old French poet), or by an occupational term (Piers Plowman), while forms like Leif Ericsson give us the start of the modern patronymic. From this beginning, the rest unfolds naturally into the wealth of family names in use today.

CHAPTER TWELVE

Your Father's Name

In the Old Testament you will very frequently find
people identified in this fashion: Isaac the son of Abraham. This is the patronymic at its purest, and has been
brought back to life in modern Israel, where David ben
Gurion is simply David the son of Gurion. The Arabs,
who are closely linked to the Hebrews by race and language, have a similar practice: Ahmed ibn Hassan is
Ahmed son of Hassan.

A variant of this system appears in the oldest Greek
writings. In the Iliad, the brothers Agamemnon and
Menelaus, leaders of the Greek forces, are often described
as the Atreidae, sons of Atreus, and Achilles is described
in the very first line of the poem as Peleiades Achileus,
Achilles son of Peleus.

In present-day Iceland there is still an old naming custom whereby Gunnar Johannssen is Gunnar son of

Johann, but Gunnar's son Eric will shift his second name to Gunnarssen, and his son in turn will bear the second name of Ericssen.

The trouble with this practice is that it does not constitute a true family name, but has to change with each generation. Early in the Middle Ages, it was found convenient to let one ancestor bestow his name upon the entire tribe and make the arrangement permanent, and so the Williamson, Johnson or Robertson which had started as a one-man patronymic became a fixed family asset to be handed on from father to son without change, regardless of the intervening first names.

In our modern practice, the original patronymic may appear in full, as in the case of Johnson or Williamson; or the -*son* may be left out, and only the first name in possessive form will appear, as in Williams, Peters, Adams, Andrews, Roberts; or the first name may be more or less telescoped, as in Jones from Johns and Davis from Davids.

Many alternatives are possible, with forms derived from abbreviated or diminutive variants as well as from the full first name. We have, for example, from the single first name Richard, such patronymics as Richardson, Dixon (Dick's son), Nixon, Dickinson, even Dickens, Dix and Hicks. Robert gives us Robertson and Roberts, but also Robbs, Hobbs and Hopkins (-*kin* is an affectionate diminutive ending added to Hob which is a corruption of Rob, which is a diminutive of Robert). Harry produces both Harrison and Harris. Some names are quite disguised by this process, and it is a regular game to try to figure out the original form. Sanders, for instance, comes from Alexander, Watson from Walter, Madison from Matt or Matthew, and Tennyson is Dennis' son. Benjamin or Ben may give us Benson, but it also occasionally turns into Bean or Beane, which is quite misleading. Another highly misleading family name is Belcher, which might at first glance be taken to be "one who belches," but turns out to be formed from the French *belle chère*, and means (descendant of) "beautiful beloved." A curious reversal of the patronymic is Bairnsfather ("child's father").

Less common is the matronymic, in which the mother supplies the name. The reverse of this is also a common practice among the Icelanders, where you find women endowed with such names as Gunnarsdatter (Gunnar's daughter), or Kristinsdatter (Christian's daughter). A common matronymic in English is Nelson (Nell's son); somewhat less frequent is Babson (Barbara's son). Scandinavian has Nansen, the name of a famous explorer. Italian has Paolo della Francesca (Paul son of Frances), who was a noted painter.

Stepping out of the Germanic into the Celtic world immediately brings to light several special patronymic prefixes, which the Celts prefer to suffixes. There is the Irish *O'* of O'Donnell, O'Hara, which does not stand for "of," but is a regular Irish form meaning "descendant of." There is the *Mc* or *Mac* (the Irish prefer the first spelling, the Scots the second), which is specifically the Gaelic word for "son." There is the *Ap-* of Welsh, exactly the same word as the *Mc* of the Irish and the *Mac* of the Scots, which is found in full form in such names as Apdavid, Aprichard, Apjones, but can also lose its initial vowel and become a mere *p-* that gives us forms like Pritchard (Aprichard, son of Richard), Price or Bryce (Aprice, son of Rice), and Bowen (Apowen, son of Owen).

A patronymic prefix first brought to England by the Normans, then passed on to the Irish is *Fitz-*, the Old French word for "son" or "son of," appearing in Fitzgerald, Fitzpatrick, Fitzsimmon, Fitzhugh.

On the European continent each language produces its own characteristic patronymic suffixes and prefixes. German has the *-sohn* of Mendelsohn, the Scandinavian languages use *-son* or *-sen* (Jansen, Amundsen, Sorensen), the Russians and Bulgarians favor an ending *-ov* or *-ev* (sometimes spelled *-off* or *-eff* in transcription), possibly a possessive plural ending, meaning "of the —s" (Ivanov, "of the Johns"; Petrov, "of the Peters"; Pavlov, "of the Pauls"; even Vinogradov, "of the grapes," and Malenkov, "of the little ones"). But Russian, along with Czech and Polish, also uses what may be described as a secondary patronymic in *-sky* or *-ski*; this is in reality an adjective ending meaning "of the nature of" (Troyansky, "Trojan," "Trojan-like"); this occasionally combines with the *-ov* or *-ev* and produces a double patronymic (Troyanovsky, "of the nature of the descendants of the Trojans," Vasilievsky, "of the nature of the descendants of the Basils"). In addition to all this, the Russians make use of a real patronymic that ends in *-ich* or *-vich*; this they use between the first name and the family name, so that Boris Fyodorovich Ivanov would mean "Boris, son of Fedor (this is really his own father's first name, and is not passed on to Boris' sons) of the Johns (a family name that does not change)." In the case of a woman, the *-vich* or -*ich* changes to -*vna*, and the -*ov* to -*ova*, so that Boris' sister Tatyana would be Tatyana Fyodorovna Ivanova. The Yugoslavs use -*ich* or -*vich* as a regular family name The Rumanians have an ending -*escu* which is often used in patronymic fashion, though it really means "pertaining to" or "like" (Antonescu, "Anthony-like," "son of Anthony").

Spanish has an ending -*ez* for family names which seems to have been originally a patronymic, so that Pérez would mean "son of Pedro" and Juánez "son of Juan"; this patronymic becomes a matronymic in Jiménez, "son of Ximena or Jimena," a woman's name. Italian prefers the word *di* or *de*, "of" (di Giovanni, de Stefano, would be the Italian equivalents of Johnson, Stevenson). French uses *de* in the same fashion, but makes relatively little use of patronymics.

The patronymic is also found in the Turkish language, where -*oglu* is frequently used. The word itself means "young man" or "boy," and the idea is that the bearer of such a name is the "boy" of the man whose name comes at the beginning. The same word for "young man" or "boy," applied in military fashion, gives rise to "uhlan," a type of lancer much in vogue in the days when the cavalry rode horses instead of tanks.

An ancient Macedonian general bore the name of Antipater, which means "against his father." Whether it is legitimate to place this name among patronymics is left to the reader's judgment.

CHAPTER THIRTEEN

Where You Live

The second great division of family names comes from the original location of the bearer. The man living on the hill might be given the name of Hill, Hills or Hillman; the one in the vicinity of the well might get to be known as Wells, Wellman, Atwell, or, with a slight change, Atwill. Church's ancestors probably lived near a church; but if the church was situated on a hill they might get to be known as Churchill. The man whose house was below the forest might become Underwood, but if he was in the forest itself it was more likely that the name would come out as Wood or Woods. Among obvious location names are Banks, Ford, Bush and Fields. Prescott is "priest's cottage."

As with the patronymic, disguised forms began to creep in quite early. Lea, Lee and Leigh would be dwellers on a lea or pastureland, but it might be a broad lea, and then the name might come out as Bradley. The same shortened form of "broad" appears in Bradstreet, Bradford and Bradhurst. *How* or *howe* is an old Anglo-Saxon name for "hill," and gives rise to our Howes; Holt is Anglo-Saxon for "wood," and is retained as a family name. Briggs is an older variant of Bridges, and Nash is "at an ash." Loughlin is from Lochland, "land of lochs or lakes."

There is a mixture of location and occupation in such names as Beebe (dweller on a bee farm) and Beasely (dweller in a field of bees). Banfield and Bancroft have to do with beans; Averill and Haverhill involve "hill" plus a word that means "oats"; Barden, Bardon, refer to a valley where barley grows, and Barlow is a barley field.

Occasionally a double interpretation is possible, as in the case of Bell, which could be a location name ("at the sign of the bell"). English inns were known by their signs, and their owners frequently acquired the name of the inn. But this name could also be of descriptive French origin (*Bel* or *Belle*), and mean "the beautiful or handsome one."

When people began living in towns and villages, the place name often led to the family name. At first there was a tendency to insert an "of" or "o'" before the place name (John of London, John o'London), but that was soon dropped, and what ultimately resulted was Jack London. In like manner we get John Hastings, Abraham Lincoln, Irving Berlin, Gaston Paris. Sometimes the city name acquires an adjective ending, particularly in those languages, like German, where the adjective bears a special ending; this appears in the name of Supreme

Court Justice Felix Frankfurter, whose ancestors must at one time have resided in the city of Frankfurt in Germany. Another American statesman who bore the name of a German city, in this case with a Latin adjective ending, was Edward Stettinius. Stettin is a city in the section of Germany now occupied by Poland; you will find it on the present map under the name of Szczecin. The -*ius* ending is not German, but Latin. Schweizer means "Swiss." The rather common name of Hess or Hesse refers to a German province, from which the Hessians came.

The town name sometimes appears in highly disguised form. Cullen, for instance, comes from Cologne or Köln, in western Germany.

During the Middle Ages, the Jews who lived in scattered communities in European countries were compelled to give up, at least for purposes of general identification, their old system of patronymics (Israel son of Abraham) and adopt permanent family names. A few chose descriptive names, or combinations of descriptive and location names, like Rothschild ("at the sign of the red shield"). For the most part, however, they favored location names of the type of Rosenfeld ("rose field") or Lilienthal ("lily valley"), or the name of the city (occasionally the country) where they lived. This was particularly true in Italy and France, with the result that certain Italian city names are used almost exclusively by members of the Italian Jewish communities (Ascoli, Piperno, d'Ancona). The French political leader Mendès-France bears the name of his country. In the eastern European lands, the Slavic patronymic suffix -*vich*, converted into -*vitz*, was often applied to a city name, with the result that we have such forms as Moscovitz, "son of Moscow."

The place name or city name is used in many languages, and numerous well-known American names today were originally foreign place names. Two of Portuguese origin are Dos Passos (this could mean "of the steps" or "of the passes") and Davega ("of the plain"; the *vega* part is the same word that appears in Las Vegas, "the plains"). The French writer Georges Duhamel bears a name that means "of the hamlet"; an even more famous French writer, Alexandre Dumas, author of *The Three Musketeers*, bore a second name which means "of the farmstead" (*mas* is a word still currently used in the south of France in the sense of "farm"). Dufour is French for "of the oven," but this could be an occupational rather than a location name, and refer to a baker. Del Río, Spanish for "of the river," has a plural variant de los Ríos, "of the rivers." Dávila is one who comes from the Spanish city of Ávila. Italians, even when not of the Jewish faith, often bear names of Italian cities: Palermo, Milano, Napoli or di Napoli; one very popular American singer, Perry Como, bears the name of a town in the extreme north of Italy, near the Swiss border. English city names, like Birmingham and Norfolk, are often borne by English speakers.

That the location-name practice was known among the ancients is shown by such names as Apuleius, a Roman writer, bearing the name of the province of Apulia. That it was common in the Middle Ages is attested by Saint Thomas Aquinas (Aquinas means "from the town of Aquino"); by Guido d'Arezzo, the monk who invented

modern musical notation (Arezzo is a town in Tuscany);
by the Italian writer Aretino (this also means "from
Arezzo"); and by the French writer Chrétien de Troyes
(Troyes is a town in France).

A sprinkling of foreign location names shows almost
exact duplication of many English forms. The French
Buisson is Bush; Dubois is "of the wood" or Woods;
Dupont is "of the bridge" or Bridges; Dupré is "of the
meadow" or Fields, as is also the case with the Spanish
de Soto and the Italian Campi. Croce, Croix, Delacroix,
de la Cruz, correspond precisely to the English Cross.
Italian Casanova is Newhouse. Spanish Calles is Streets,
and comes close to our Streeter. A few names that do
not have an exact equivalent in English are the German
Berger ("mountaineer") and Bürger ("townsman"); the
Italian Fontana, French la Fontaine, Spanish Fuentes
("fountain" or "spring"); Spanish Huerta ("garden") and
Villa (either "town" or "country estate"). Montagu, a
name that has taken deep root in English, is originally
French for "sharp peak." Richelieu, the name of a famous
French cardinal and statesman, is "rich place." Torque-
mada, founder of the Spanish Inquisition, is "burned
tower."

Even in an Oriental language like Chinese the place
name is common. Pei, meaning "north," appears in numerous Chinese place names (Pei-ho, the North River, Pei-
King or Peking, the Northern Capital, Pei-ping, "northern
peace"); in slightly different form, it is also an extremely
common Chinese family name, just as North frequently
appears in English-speaking lands.

CHAPTER FOURTEEN

The Name of Your Trade

If a man is to be distinguished by the name of his trade or occupation, then it is fairly obvious that the occupations most frequently represented in family names would be the ones current at the time when family names began. Hence we find a predominance of Smiths, Taylors, Bakers, Brewers, Coopers, Barbers (Barbours), together with a somewhat smaller representation of Clarks, Schreibers (German for "writer"), Lerners (German for "student"), Priests (or Priestleys), and practically no Scientists or Engineers. This is also the reason for a very frequent occurrence of names of trades that have practically disappeared, like Fletcher (arrow maker). Lastly, this is why the trade name is one of constant, almost infinite repetition from one language to another, so that Smith can be translated into a hundred other tongues and find itself perfectly at home, while the English Baker

86

(or Baxter) can go on to the German Becker, the French Boulanger, the Italian Fornari or Fornaciari, and similar equivalents in all countries where bread and not rice is the staff of life.

Another thing which strikes us is the relatively high degree of specialization within certain trades indicated by family names. We have not only Smith, but also Goldsmith, Silversmith (or Silvermaster), Arrowsmith. The last name points to the importance of the specialized armorer in a medieval society geared for almost constant warfare. There is the Fletcher which comes straight from the Old French *fléchier*, "arrow maker," which in turn comes from *flèche*, "arrow." There is Boyer, the man who makes or sells bows. Then there is the Archer or Bowman, the one who actually uses the bow. There is the Armor or Armour or Armbruster who is the maker of armor. There is the originally German Kefauver, the maker of lances or javelins (although the *-fauver* part comes from the Latin *faber*, "smith"). There is the Eisenhower, or iron-hewer, whose German name is the exact equivalent of the French Taillefer that ultimately becomes Taliaferro and Tolliver. There is the Farrier or Farrar, who is the French *ferrier*, again "smith." In Italy you can come across names like Arcaro ("bowmaker") and Arcieri ("bowman"), along with a Gaida that originally meant "spear," and a couple of common Sicilian names that come from Arabic, like Morabito and Mugavero, which mean "spearman" or "javelin thrower." Shields is duplicated by the Italian Scutaro. Farragut was originally a Catalonian name meaning "sharp iron" or "sword." To one who reads between the lines it becomes fairly obvious that the society which originally evolved those names was one where war and its implements played an important role.

That all was not war, however, is indicated by the appearance of many peaceful occupations also. German has a large number of Bauers ("farmer"; a name common also among English speakers), with the variants Bauman, Baumann, Baumgartner (the last is "tree gardener"). There is an English Barker (really a tanner), a Barger (one who works on a barge), a Badger (not an animal, but one who buys products in one place and transports them to another place to sell). Bellman is one employed to go around the streets of a town with a bell to make public announcements; Bleecker bleaches cloth; Bolger makes leather wallets or bags; Boardman hews boards. Carpenter needs no explanation; he is paralleled by the French Charpentier, the German Zimmermann, the Hungarian Asztalos, and dozens of other forms in as many languages. Taylor and the older Snyder ("cutter") are paralleled by the German Schneider, the French Sartre, the Italian Sarto or del Sarto.

Brewer takes numerous variant forms, some English, some Dutch, some German: Brewster, Brauer, Brower, Breyer, Breier, Breuer. Our Cooper (one who makes casks or barrels) has German variants like Boettcher and Boettger. These two names alone indicate a certain interest in the product of the brewing and wine-making process, natural enough in the days of no coffee, no tea, no chocolate, and no Coca Cola.

Royalty, nobility and high Church offices seem to be widely represented in such forms as King, Noble, Duke,

Abbott, Pope and Bishop (Italian has Conti and Nobile, French has Lecomte and Leduc); but here we must remember that these names often go back to morality plays and the players who filled assigned roles. Even Blessing comes from one who personified the blessing in such plays. A few authentically religious names appear among the Jews, where Cohen is "priest," Schochat is "sacrificial butcher," and Meier is "teacher."

Numerous occupational names need no explanation: Arkwright, Bricker, Butler, Tyler, Carman, Carter, Constable, Cook, Draper, Forester, Fowler, Glover, Marshall, Mason, Stewart (or Stuart, from "steward"). Chamberlin or Chamberlain, too, is self-explanatory. For some, a word of clarification is in order. Chapman is an archaic word for merchant, and corresponds to the German Kaufman. Collier comes from "coal" (we still speak of a colliery). Currier could be either an English form of the French Courier ("courier"), or one who curries horses. Palmer is one who sold palm branches at religious festivals. Chaucer is the French *chaussier*, a maker of footwear.

Some common occupational names of non-English origin in our midst are the German Wagner ("wagoner"), Wassermann ("waterman"), Weber ("weaver"); the Spanish Romero ("pilgrim"); the French Pasteur ("shepherd" or "pastor"), Lemaître ("the teacher" or "the master"), Lepage ("the page"), Boucher ("butcher"); the Italian Alfieri ("standard bearer"), La Guardia ("the guard"), Medici ("physician"), Ghirlandajo ("wreath maker"), Finocchiaro ("fennel grower" or "fennel seller").

With the possible exception of Smith, no name has a

greater international range than Miller (German Müller, Italian Molinari, French Meunier or Desmoulins, Hungarian Molnar, Czech Mlinar, etc.). Franklin is a "freeman"; he is to some extent paralleled by the Italian Liberati and Liberace, though this is descriptive of a condition rather than an occupation.

Returning for an instant to the metal trades, we find Hammarskjold ("hammer shield") in Scandinavian and Molotov ("of the hammers") in Russian. Yet it must be remembered that Hammer when it appears in a German name refers not to the tool, but to a dweller on the pasture ground.

In the matter of original derivations, Smith goes back to a root *smēi*, which means "to work with a sharp tool." The original Anglo-Saxon form seems to have meant specifically "wheel maker," which would make Smith the equivalent of Wright and Cartwright. The Russian counterpart of Smith, Kuznetsov, comes from a root *kāu*, "to hew or strike," which actually appears in our "hew," as well as, strangely, in our "code" and "codicil."

CHAPTER FIFTEEN

Names of Description, Glory and Shame

Descriptive names form perhaps a majority of our total stock of family names, and among them those descriptive of color of hair, skin or complexion seem to predominate. English has Black (or Blake), Brown, White, Green, Gray, and even Bay ("the man with the reddish-brown hair"), but these are only the obvious ones. Concealed in Russell, Reid and Read lies "red"; concealed in Blank lies a French *blanc*, "white." Bowie is one with yellow or fair hair; Gwyn, Wynne, Baine, Bean, Beane, are all Celtic forms of White, and even Bannon or Bannion is "the little white one." Morris and its patronymic Morrison, Morrell, Morse, all come from "Moor" or dark-complexioned, and Dunn is another form meaning "dark." One interesting item about Blake is that it can come from either of two Anglo-Saxon words, *blæc* meaning "black" or *blæcan*, meaning "to bleach or make white" (the idea is really the same—depriving an object of color; only the outcomes are opposite).

Another feature of the color names is that they are fully international. Our White is paralleled by French Leblanc, Italian Bianchi or Lobianco, Spanish Alvarez, German Weiss, Slavic Bialas, Bialy, Bialek. For Black there is the French Lenoir, the Italian Neri, Negro, de Negri, the German Schwartz, the Dutch Zwart. For Brown there is the French Lebrun, the German Braun, for Green the Italian Verdi and the Slavic Zelenko, for our various "Moor" forms you have Maurois, Mauriac, Morelli, Moretti, Mauro. For our names that come from "red" you have Rossi, Rossini, Rossetti, Rosselli, Leroux, Rojas, even Scarlatti. French and Spanish have even a Doré and Dorado for our Golden, and German has a Gelb, "yellow," that we seem to lack.

Descriptions of physical qualities are just as numerous and just as international. We have Long and Lang, and so have most other languages. Our Young is paralleled by French Lejeune, and its opposite, Olds, by Italian Vecchi. We sometimes speak jokingly of "Mr. Big," forgetting that Mr. Grant and Mr. More mean just that; one comes from French, the other from Celtic. They are paralleled by French Legrand, Italian Grandi, German Gross, Hungarian Nagy. For our Little there is the Italian Lopiccolo, the Hungarian Kis, the Russian Malenkov. Our Bass comes from French and means "short"; Italian has Bassi, and even Grassi, which is our Stout.

A few other physical characteristics taken at random might include our Armstrong and Beauregard (originally French for "good look"), the Italian Bellini ("pretty"), the Russian Borodin ("bearded"). Then there are names descriptive of moral qualities, like Blythe, Bliss, Moody, or the Bonner, Bonney and Bunch that all come from the French *bon*, "good." (Italian has Bonomo, German has Gutmann or Gutermann, and we also have Good and Goodman.) Bellamy is the French *bel ami*, "fair (or fine) friend."

Our Wise is equalled by French Lesage and Italian Losavio. Hebrew has Baruch ("blessed"), Russian has Gorky ("bitter"), Italian has Gentile ("gentle"), Amati ("beloved"), Pacifici ("peaceful"), Angelici ("angelic"). The Spanish Cortés is "polite," and Coronado is "crowned." It may be noticed that French and Italian names often bring out the original nickname feature better than ours, since they usually prefix "the" to the adjective (Lejeune, "the young one," vs. English Young).

Even attire, activity, political affiliation and religion come into the picture of family names. Capablanca, greatest chess player of all time, is "white cloak." Doolittle is self-explanatory. Bonaparte is "on the right side," and Mindszenty, the Hungarian hero cardinal, is "All Saints." Smetana, the Czech composer, is "cream" in Slavic, and Bronte, the manufactured name of a family of English lady novelists, is Greek for "thunder." An ethical principle, or perhaps a stomach disorder, appears in Drinkwater, for which the French is Boileau and the Italian Bevilacqua.

Race and nationality appear frequently. Such names as French, Norman, Saxon, Allen, Britton or Britten, Picard, Fleming, Lombard, Scott, Holland or Hollander, Welsh or Walsh, are all indicative of a place of origin.

A curiously concealed name of this sort is Langley, which is the English corruption of the French *l'Anglais*, "the Englishman." Nimitz conceals the Slavic word for "German" (Nemetz). Böhm or Böhmer is the German word for "Bohemian," which we would today call Czech. Czech itself appears in Chekhov, "of the Czechs," the name of a famous Russian writer. The first part of the name of Rimsky-Korsakov, the Russian composer, means "Roman." Török, a common Hungarian family name, means "Turk." The name of the former Mexican President Alemán means "German" in Spanish. The Spanish dictator Franco may be "frank" or "Frankish." In Italian such names as Tudisco ("German"), Russo ("Russian"), Franchi ("Frank"), Romano ("Roman"), are quite common. The name of the French Premier de Gaulle may be an indication of Gaulish origin.

Animal names also abound. It has been estimated that three per cent of all family names in English are of this nature (Hogge, Crabbe, Beaver, with Beaverbrook, Beverly and Beveridge, Crane, Lion, Cox, Fox, Fish, with its Scandinavian variant Fiske, etc.). We even find a Jack Rabbits on a college football team.

Most popular among animal names in family form is Bear. It appears in the variants Baer, Behr, Bahr, and in compound forms like Barnhart, Barnard, Barrett, Behrens, Barnett. Wolf or Wolfe is almost as popular, with Wolfson, Adolfson, and similar forms. Adler and Ahrens both have to do with an eagle, and the originally German Auer or Auermann with a bison, while Agnew is connected with lamb, and Ahearn is "horse owner." Best often comes from "beast," and has the French Labiche as its parallel (it must be remembered that these animal names often refer to a sign on an inn rather than to the animal itself). Among foreign animal names one could mention the Slavic Sokolsky, connected with hawk or falcon, the Italian Tasso, with means "badger," Leopardi, "leopard," Pecora, "sheep," and Vespucci, who gave his first name to America, and whose second name means "little wasps." Most picturesque among foreign animal names is that of the Italian composer of the opera *Cavalleria Rusticana*, Leoncavallo, which means "Horse Lion."

There are a few nicknames which might be described as belonging to the second rather than to the first name class. Among these are the Spanish explorer Cabeza de Vaca (the name means "Cow head"; his real name was Alvar Núñez), the Italian painter Cimabue ("Oxtop" translates it), the German Emperor Frederick Barbarossa ("Redbeard"), and the French-born American essayist Crèvecoeur (the name means "Heartbreak"). Other names lend themselves to international punning. Liebig, for instance, is connected with the idea of "love" in German, but if it is broken up into two English syllables, the meaning is quite different. Lever, which could refer to a tool in English (it is more probable that it goes back to a French Levert, "Green") would, if spelled in its present English form, mean "the Worm" in French.

One category of names, by reason of historical connotations, has grown into a series of glorifying terms on the one hand, of opprobrious epithets on the other. Calling someone a Jefferson or a Lincoln would be quite a compliment; calling him a Benedict Arnold would be something else. Quisling was a Norwegian statesman who collaborated with the Nazis; calling someone a Quisling is equivalent to calling him a traitor or double crosser. In like manner, we may call someone a Hitler (or Schickelgruber), a Nero, or an Attila ("the Scourge of God"). But to call a military leader a Napoleon or a Julius Caesar is to endow him with the highest attributes of his calling.

Similar terms exist in all lands. A Bolívar in Latin America, a Garibaldi in Italy, would be the equivalents of a George Washington in the United States.

The name Garibaldi means "war bold," and contains the same root that appears in our "bold" and in the name of the Scandinavian god Baldur. Columbus comes from a Latin word meaning "dove," but there is some doubt as to whether the original root is one meaning "spotted or gray" or one meaning "to shimmer." The name of Tolstoi, author of *War and Peace*, goes back to a root that means "thick or swollen"; the same root appears in our "stalactite" and "stalagmite." Strauss, the famous composer of the "Blue Danube," bears a name whose root means "stiff" or "strife," which appears also in "strenuous," "stern" and "starve" (but it may also come from other roots meaning "flower bunch" or "ostrich"). Ohm, the German scientist after whom the electrical unit of resistance is named, bears a name that means "grandfather" or "uncle," and is closely related to the antiquated English "eam" or "eme." Two other German names of fairly frequent occurrence have a descriptive force. One is Reuter, from a root meaning "to grab up or snatch," appearing also in "ruin," "rough" and "robber."

The other is Geisel, which means "hostage," from a root meaning "security" or "pledge."

Family names, as we see, are as thoroughly meaningful as first names. They, too, tell a story, but it is one that often occurs so far back in time as to have little or no connotation value today.

CHAPTER SIXTEEN

The Commonest Names

One study made some years ago revealed that by far the most common family name in the English-speaking world is Smith, with or without its variants (Smythe, Smithson, Smithfield, etc.). Since the picture in the United States is somewhat clouded by the large number of names of non-English origin, the British results will perhaps give a clearer indication of the situation. The list of contributors to the British National Savings Scheme (a distant relative of our Social Security) included 290,-000 Smiths, 200,000 Joneses, 150,000 Browns, and 130,-000 Williamses.

A similar study made in Scotland gave the Smiths as 16 per 1,000 population. Here the runners-up were not Joneses, Browns and Williamses, but MacDonalds (12 per 1,000 population) and Campbells (10 per 1,000).

In Ireland, where the Celtic tradition is stronger, the

Smiths ran fifth, being topped by the Murphys, Kellys, Sullivans, and Walshes. Following Smith, however, were such popular Irish names as O'Brien, Byrne, Ryan, Connor, O'Neill, Reilly, Doyle, McCarthy, Gallagher and Doherty.

In America, despite the presence of numerous immigrant names, Smith still runs first, with Johnson, Brown, Jones and Wilson following.

This predominance of an occupational name can only be attributed to historical conditions; specifically, to the importance of the smith in a medieval civilization in which he represented the chief form of mechanization. This supposition is borne out by the picture found in other languages of the western world. The Germanic languages use a word similar to Smith (German Schmidt, Dutch Smit). The Romance tongues have words that contain the Latin root for "iron", *ferrum.* In French you have Ferrier and Ferry, along with a southern French form Ferrar or Farrar. Spanish has Herrero, Herrera and the Catalonian Ferrer. Italian uses Ferraro, Ferrari, Ferri. Hungarian has Kovacs, Polish has Kowalski, Russian has Kuznetsov. Even the Arab world has its Smith in the form of Haddad. Then there are all sorts of kindred names dealing with the smith's occupation, like Bellows, or the French Laforge, Lafarge.

Some years ago a New York newspaper ran a series of articles about the name of Smith and its intricate ramifications. There was, for instance, the drive by Smith College to invite all people named Smith and the inhabitants of all Smithfields, Smithtowns and Smithvilles to contribute to its endowment and thus help perpetuate the name (Smithfield, however, does not get its name from Smith, but from "smooth"). All sorts of strange first name combinations have been devised to give individual Smiths individuality, among them 5/8 Smith, Xenophon Smith, Zemro Smith, Lung Smith, Nevada Smith, Erasmus Peshine Smith, Coffin Smith, and even William McKinley Louisiana Levee Bust Smith and Loyal Lodge No. 296 Knights of Pythias Ponca City Oklahoma Smith.

No other name in common use, apparently, causes so much confusion, though there is a tale about two C. E. Wilsons, one of whom was president of General Electric, the other president of General Motors. The nicknames "Good Evening" Wilson and "Good Morning" Wilson were coined for them.

Smith, Jones and Johnson are among the very common American family names that have also become common in parts of the non-English-speaking world. The city of Cárdenas, in Cuba, has a large sprinkling of native-born Smiths, Joneses, Johnsons and Hubbards. They are the descendants of Americans, mainly from New England, who came to Cuba in the early eighteenth century in connection with the molasses trade. It is of interest that the name Jones down there, pronounced in accordance with the Spanish rules, comes out as HOH-nays. Another large colony of Smiths, Joneses, Beauregards and kindred names appears in Brazil, where the bearers are descendants of Confederate die-hards who preferred emigration to another land to submission to the will of the North.

The frequency of occurrence of given family names in other languages is not quite so easy to determine,

partly because of lack of statistics, often because of vast
dialectal differences which lead to the frequent use of
one name in one part of the country and to its being
practically ignored elsewhere, sometimes because of
variants like those that appear in Smith, Smythe and
Smithson.

Among German names, colors predominate, but they
are often in combination with other words. Names in
which Schwarz ("black"), Weiss ("white"), Roth ("red"),
Braun ("brown"), Grün ("green"), appear are extremely
frequent. Other very popular forms are Gross ("big") and
Klein ("little"), Mayer or Meyer, Baum ("tree"), Blume
("flower"), Stein ("stone"), Stern ("star"), Gold ("gold"),
Silber ("silver"), Katz ("cat"), Fried ("peace"), Hirsch
("deer"), Rosen ("rose"), Wein ("wine"), Kaufman ("merchant"). The popularity of most of these forms also
among non-German but Yiddish-speaking Jews confuses
the picture. Names less likely to appear in Jewish groups
are occupational names of the type of Fischer, Müller,
Schneider, Zimmermann, Schmidt, Richter, Schäfer,
Singer, Wagner, Weber, Graf (respectively "fisher,"
"miller," "tailor," "carpenter," "smith," "judge," "maker,"
"singer," "carter," "weaver," "count"); such animal names
as Wolf, Haas ("hare"), Vogel ("bird"), Hahn ("rooster");
location names like Pomerantz ("Pomeranian"), Wald or
Walde ("forest"), Brück or Brücke ("bridge"), Sachs
("Saxony"), Hess or Hesse ("Hesse"), Schlesinger ("Sile-
sian"); and others like Schultz, Neumann and Strauss.

The two most popular Jewish names are Cohen, which
is occupational, meaning "priest," and Levy (with all its
variants Levi, Levin, Levine, Levinson, etc.), which may

be described as a tribal name. Kaplan, corresponding to our "chaplain," but having rather the meaning of "priest's assistant," is also frequent.

The Scandinavian groups run heavily to patronymics of the type of Anderson, Hanson, Jansen, Larson, Olsen, Sorensen, Jorgensen, Rasmussen. Lind, Lund and Tietjen are also of very frequent occurrence. Dutch has a fondness for Schuyler and for patronymics with the prefix *van* (Van Dyk, Vandenberg, Van Raalte, etc.).

The patronymic predominates in Spanish, with such names as Rodríguez, Fernández or Hernández, González, Martínez, Pérez, López. Popular location names are Rivera ("river bank") and Torres ("towers"). Díaz and Ortiz are of frequent occurrence.

French has a fondness for location names of the type of Dumont, Dupré, Dupont ("of the mountain," "of the meadow," "of the bridge"), and occupational names like Leclerc, Lemaître ("the scribe," "the teacher"), or, without the article, Lanier ("wool worker") or Pelletier ("worker in skins"). Names of regions (Picard, Le Breton, Lenormand) and names derived from first names, which may or may not be patronymics (Jacques, Jacquier, Jacquet, Jacquot, Michel, François), are also frequent.

Portuguese goes in heavily for location names of the type of Costa, Ponte and Silva ("coast," "bridge," "wood"; these may appear with or without a prefixed *A-* or *Da-*, as in Dacosta, Aponte). Other popular Portuguese forms are Pereira, Figueira and Andrade.

The Italian frequency picture is obscured by dialectal factors, with each region forming its own names, which often have unmistakable characteristics (a name ending in -*ddu* or -*dda*, for instance, is almost sure to be Sardinian, while one ending in -*illo* is pretty definitely Neapolitan). Two names of frequent occurrence, both showing southern features, are Russo (which may mean "Russian," but is more likely to be the southern variant of Rosso, "red"), and Esposito, which means "foundling." Marino ("pertaining to the sea") is rather frequent, but more likely to be southern or Sicilian than northern. Rosa (La Rosa, De or Di Rosa), Rosso, Rossi, Rossini, Rossetti, all have to do with "rose" or "red." Fiore, "flower," in a very large number of variants, is common throughout Italy. So are Mazza ("club or stick") and Pace ("peace"). Romano and Lombardo are popular location names. Patronymics with *di* or *de* ("of") are extremely common (de Martino, di Giacomo, etc.).

Among Slavic names there is a predominance of patronymics in -*ov* and -*ev*, particularly in Russian (Ivanov, Pavlov, Petrov, Popov; the last means "of the priests," *pop* being the Russian word for "priest"). Janow would be the Polish equivalent of the Russian Ivanov, roughly translatable as Johnson or Jones. Ostrov, however, despite its seeming patronymic ending, means "island." Dubin and Dubinsky have to do with a cudgel or an oak grove. Krasny and its variants (Krasner, Krasov, etc.) contain a root which is either "red" or "beautiful," according to the particular language in which it appears. Golub is perhaps the favorite Slavic animal name; it means "dove." Sirota and its variants have the meaning of "orphan." Polak and its variants, such as Pollock, are location names, meaning "Polish," while the very common Czech name Novak contains the root of "new."

Hungarian names of considerable frequency are Farkas ("wolf"), Nagy ("big"), Kovács ("smith"), Molnár ("miller"), Németh, Horváth and Szabó. By far the most common modern Greek name is Pappas, which is often an abbreviation of a longer name, like Pappageotes. Like the Russian *pop*, this indicates descent from a priest of the Eastern Church, which allows its priests to marry. Descriptive names like Makris ("long") and Mavros ("dark complexioned") are frequent in Greek; so are patronymics like Demetriou and national names like Vlahos ("from Wallachia," or "belonging to the Wallachian group in Macedonia").

One of the most popular Japanese names is Suzuki, which means "bell-tree." Saito, names beginning with Yama- "mountain" (Yamada, Yamashita), and names ending in -mura, "village" (Nakamura, Nishimura) are also common. In the Chinese world, there is a dialectal factor to be considered. Names ending in consonants other than -*n* or -*ng*, like Nip or Lok, are usually of southern Chinese (Cantonese) origin, since the official Mandarin of northern China does not, as a rule, have consonant endings other than the two mentioned. Among popular Chinese family names are Wong, Yi, Chan, Chang, Chen, Cheng, Chu, Leung and Ng. By far the most popular Korean family name is Kim.

CHAPTER SEVENTEEN

The Long, the Short, the Funny

Shortest among family names, at least in written form, is an authentic Monsieur O, from France. There are at least two common family names in Chinese, however, which, though transcribed by two letters, consist of a single consonant sound; they are Ng and Sz (the latter, for the sake of convenience in pronouncing, is often transcribed as Sze). Other names consisting of a single letter of the alphabet appear, but they seem to have been deliberately manufactured by their owners. There is, for example, the story of a Milwaukee woman who applied to the courts to restore her maiden name of Montgomery in connection with her divorce suit against her husband, Jerry X. The Social Security rolls contain numerous family names appearing as X, Y and Z, and, in lesser numbers, all the other letters of the alphabet with the exception (we wonder why) of C, J, O, Q and W. They also contain such one-syllable names as Oz, Hah, and Ugh. Since Chinese words all consist of a single syllable, it is no trick at all to find short names in Chinese, such as Li or Wu. One of the shortest first and second name combinations on record is the full name of the former Premier of Burma (Burmese belongs to the same language family as Chinese, and also uses one-syllable words); the name is U Nu.

At the other end of the line are Polish names like Grzeszczyszyn (pronounced, if you care to try, Gsheshchishin) and Konstantynopolitanczkowski, and Japanese names like Kurumabayashi. The longest names on record, however, come from Thailand, Hawaii and the Fiji Islands. The full name of the crown prince who will one day inherit the crown of Thailand (Siam) is Vajiralongkorn Boromchadrayadisorn Santatiwong Thevetthamrong Suboribarn Abhigunooprakarnmahitladuldej Phumiphonnaveretvarangkur Kittosirisom-Booranasawangkawadh Boromkattiyarajkumar.

Hawaii counters with a nickname used by a local politician, which runs Keliilikalakalakekeikiokuanaoa, as well as with an authentic name, borne by an accounting department clerk, which makes a signature on a check a practical impossibility: Floyd Kuikealakauaokalani Kealiiwailanamalie Kamanunuihalakaipo Hoopii. Lastly, the Fiji Islands give the name of a local assistant superintendent of police as Levani V. Tamanikairukurukuiovalau.

Some family names are striking by reason of their actual meaning, like the Italian La Morte ("death"), or Criminale ("criminal"), or the English Bed, Knee, Leg, Shiner, Zipper, Lip, Kiss, Hug and Garter, all of which, preceded by the initial A., turned up at one time or another on a TV program that specializes in names. Others are striking only by reason of first and second name combination, like Virginia Ham, June Bride, June Wedding and June Bug. The same program has had at various times people named B. O. Plenty, Dick Tracy, Donald Duck, Joe Palooka, Andie and Minnie Gump, Kris Kringle, William Tell, Sherlock Holmes, Julius Caesar, George Washington, and Francis A. Mule, along with male Gene Tierneys and Shirley Temples, and a Peter Rabbit who proved to be a married man with a large family. Having made a study of familiar names, the program director confidently asserts that there are living today in the United States at least four hundred Robert Taylors, three hundred Mary Martins, and the same number of Helen Hayeses, together with numerous Faye Emersons and Elsa Maxwells.

Sometimes the striking feature is brought about by a combination of two persons, as when Flesh and Blood (Charles Flesh and Chic Blood) worked together in a Memphis air-lines office, or by a combination of a personal and a place name, as in the case of Penny Nichols from Money, Miss. At other times the striking feature comes from a foreign name which has an entirely different meaning in English from what it has in the original language, as in the case of Ingo Waste from Klagenfurt, Austria; it is probable that the Kiss listed above may not be the English "kiss," but the Hungarian *kis*, meaning "little."

Lastly, there are the deliberately contrived names, like Roy Takencareof, who was actually taken care of in the

county jail of Grafton, N. D., where he went AWOL
from the Army, or the Georgia Alabama Florida (a man),
who explained his rather curious name on the ground
that his father's name was Joe Florida, his mother's name
was Georgianna, and he was born on a showboat tied up
at Mobile, Ala. The Social Security lists mentioned above
report such names as Name, Names, Odear, Oboy and
Ostop, along with Aaaaa and Zyzys, and it is difficult to
escape the suspicion that they are deliberately contrived
for effect, like the Good Knight assumed by one man
whose second name was really Knight, or the imaginary
Guy de Nouement, claimed to be a French author of
mystery stories. There is the Captain Nemo (Latin for
"no one") first devised by Jules Verne for his *Twenty
Thousand Leagues Under the Sea*, and later appropri-
ated by our comic strips. There is also a Mrs. Gotrocks,
used to describe a woman of considerable wealth, a Lady
Bountiful, who adds generosity to wealth, and the Cas-
par Milquetoast used to indicate a man of excessive
timidity. Boniface, the name of a literary personage, is
often applied to an innkeeper.

The deliberately contrived name with subtler features
is claimed by one literary expert to have been used to
good effect by Dickens in his novels, with the use of the
vowel *i* to betoken timidity, as in the case of Fips, Grig
and Sniggs, of the vowel *u* to symbolize clumsiness, as in
Nuff, Bumble and Bugby, and of a combination of the
two vowel sounds to indicate a mixture of the two qualities, as in Nupkins and Spruggins.

Whether this vowel symbolism be a correct interpretation or not, there is no question that authors have fre-

quently contrived names for their characters with a view to predisposing their readers to the unfolding of the actions of those characters. Ariosto has in one of his poems a boastful Algerian king named Rodomonte (literally "I gnaw the mountain"), whose name is a dead giveaway even before he speaks; it has given rise to "rodomontade" in English. Elsewhere we find a Captain Fracassa (the word means "smashes") who actually smashes everything in his path. One of the most far-reaching results for a contrived name was achieved by Plautus, a Roman comedy writer of the third century B. C., who created a character who ate everything in sight and gave him the name of Manducus, formed from Latin roots meaning "to lead (up to the mouth) with the hand" (another explanation is that it comes from *mandibula*, "mandible" or "jaw"). This character proved so popular with the Roman theater-going audiences that on the basis of his name they built up a verb *manducare*, which at first meant "to eat greedily," then simply "to eat." This slang verb, displacing the original Latin word for "to eat" (*edere*) in some parts of the Roman Empire, ultimately emerged as the regular word for "to eat" in French and Italian (*manger, mangiare*).

It is interesting to note the fashion in which some languages express the idea conveyed by the English "so-and-so." German has the same expression (*so und so*). French uses *un tel*, "a such." Italian has *il tal dei tali*, "the such of suches." Spanish uses *fulano*, a word from Arabic, often with the addition of *de tal*, "of such." Spanish also uses the rhyming Fulano, Sutano y Mengano in the sense of our "Tom, Dick and Harry."

CHAPTER EIGHTEEN

Pronunciation and Spelling Problems

It is well known that some English names do not sound at all like their written forms. This begins with names like Auchinleck, Leicester, Gloucester, Beauchamps, pronounced Aflek, Lester, Gloster, Beecham, and reaches its culmination in the pronounced rendering of a British telephone number, Cholmondeley 1100, which you give to the operator as "Chumley, double one, double naught." A few of these atrocities have crossed the ocean, so that even here we have Taliaferro pronounced as Tolliver and Wemyss pronounced as Weems. Americans, however, show a strong tendency to reform the spelling when its pronunciation diverges too greatly from it, as shown by Wooster from Worcester.

It is non-English names that cause some of the worst headaches. What to do, for instance, with the German-Jewish names in *-stein*: pronounce them as in "beer

stein," or as -*steen*? Fried, the German name that contains the root of "peace," should come out as "freed," but
is occasionally given as in "fried eggs." Spanish names
like Jiménez, Rodríguez, Martínez, should carry the stress
on the next to the last syllable, but are often given out
with initial stress, and de Jesús, which should sound day-
hay-SOOS, is regularly given the English pronunciation
for "Jesus." Contrariwise, Italian names like Esposito and
Pecora, which have stress on the third syllable from the
end, are given stress on the penult. French and German
names often coincide with English forms, so the transition is easy, but with Slavic names it is almost anybody's
guess. One name that perhaps gave more trouble than
any other until at least its spelling became fixed in the
American mind is that of Khrushchev. The sound is something else again; not too many newscasters pronounce it
correctly as khroosh-CHAWV. Van Gogh should, but
seldom does, come out as Van Khokh.

It is consoling to think that similar problems arise in
other lands when English names are attempted. We have
already seen the Spanish-speaking Cubans pronouncing
Jones as HOH-nays. In their transcription of American
names into Cyrillic characters, the Russians invariably
transcribe our H as a G, so that Hillman comes out as
Gillman in their spelling and pronunciation. This is due
to the fact that there is in Russian no true equivalent for
our *h*-sound. The two sounds that come closest are *g* and
kh, and of the two, they prefer the former.

A very amusing news item from Brazil tells us of what
happens down there to the sound of some of our widely

advertised products. Colgate is not understood in its normal English pronunciation, but becomes readily accessible if you say Coal-GAH-tchey. In like manner, some of our best-known automobile brands become FOR-jey; BOO-eek, OOD-song and Ply-MOO-chee. MAR-lin Mo-HOY, TAW-ney HOO-sell, Hey Meel-UND and AID-ward HOB-by-soon are the pronounced forms of Marilyn Monroe, Tony Russell, Ray Milland and Edward Robinson. The Avenida Churchill in Rio is Sure-SHILL.

Best of all, however, is what happens to English names in Japanese and Chinese transcription and pronunciation. Since the Japanese language normally permits only syllables consisting of consonant plus vowel, and does not have the sound of *l*, a name like Clark comes out as Ku-ra-ku, with *r* substituting for *l*, the original *r* of Clark dispensed with, and vowels inserted after each consonant sound.

In Chinese the problem is different. Here it is a matter of rendering the pronunciation in Chinese words of one syllable, strung together. Since these words have definite meanings in Chinese, the combination that comes out is often very interesting. At the time of one Presidential election, Stevenson and Eisenhower were rendered as follows: Sz Ti Wen Sen (meaning: history brings literary life), and Ai Sen How Wei (meaning: love jungle hero manliness). This was the fashion in which the problem was solved by the Nationalist Chinese on Formosa. The Communist Chinese on the mainland gave a slightly different version, with the meaning "history flower-base literary forest" for the Democratic candidate, and "ivy jungle hero manliness you" for the Republican.

Three other names of international figures that come out into interesting Chinese combinations are Hammarskjold, Ha Ma Show, ("hello horse introduction"), Lodge, Lo Chee ("river wonderful"), and Vishinsky ("but bitter this foundation").

Where languages use the same alphabet but different letter combinations to indicate similar sounds, there is often a deliberate change of spelling. An Italian Amici, for instance, may appear as Ameche (Ameechee would be even closer to the original pronunciation). Hungarian Szell and Szabó are often modified into Sell and Sabo. The German ending *-stein* is sometimes changed to *-stine* or *-steen*, according to the pronunciation wanted. We have already seen a French *l'Anglais* turn into Langley; in like manner, Leclerc often becomes Leclair.

It is a little difficult to give advice on what to do in the matter of pronouncing foreign names. In cases where the name has been fully assimilated into American life, and its bearer is American-born, there is little point in trying to render the original pronunciation. Schuyler and Dupont do not sound precisely the same in Dutch and French as they do in America; but the Schuylers and the Duponts have been here a long time, and the original pronunciation would seem strange even to their ears. On the other hand, when the name is borne by a foreign national, our mispronunciation will sound about as bad as the Spanish HOH-nays for Jones. It is also true, however, that neither we nor the foreigners can be expected to master the rules of pronunciation of all the languages in existence. For radio announcers and newscasters there are manuals of pronunciation available giving reasonable approximations to the names of people frequently in the news. For the rest of us, perhaps the most practical advice is to struggle along and do the best we can.

CHAPTER NINETEEN

Naming Customs

We have seen that the English-speaking world often uses family names as first names. The contrary practice, of using first names as family names, is fairly international. To some extent, this is a direct outcome of the patronymic form of family name. Often, however, there is no visible sign of a patronymic. This is the case with such English family names as Lewis and Owen, French names like Michel and François, German names like Bernhardt and Eberhard.

There are other name customs which are typical of the English speakers. While it is a general international practice for a woman to assume her husband's family name, it is not at all general for her to assume his first name as well (Mrs. George Jones, for instance, instead of Mrs. Charlotte Jones). This leads to another practice, that of labelling a couple as the Frank Browns, or the

James Mortons. This custom is said by some to stifle a woman's individuality, and there is even a society, known as the Lucy Stoners, who try to uphold the principle that a married woman should retain her maiden name. In many cases nowadays, a woman's name is well known before marriage, and she is compelled to retain it for business reasons. Elizabeth Arden and Pearl Buck are two clear-cut examples. It is sometimes claimed that the woman's use of her own first name indicates that she is either widowed or divorced, but this usage is far from having general acceptance, and Emily Post frowns on it.

It is a vogue in American radio interviewing to give the full name to the interviewee, rather than to address him as "Mr." followed by his family name. This is obviously in the interest of precise identification by the audience, but may eventually affect conversational practice.

In a good many countries it is customary to put the family name before the given name. This is true, among others, of Hungary (Kossuth Lajos, for the man we would know as Louis Kossuth) and China (Chiang Kai-shek, which is really Kai-shek of the Chiang family). In official Italian records, it is customary for the family name to come first, followed by the given name, then the father's name preceded by *di* ("of") if the father is still living, by *fu* ("was") if the father is dead.

In Iceland, where the sole second name is a true patronymic (Olafur Halldorsson, "Olaf, son of Halldor"), listing in the telephone directory is under first names only. The directory helps you out, though, by giving the subscriber's title or profession. This listing of titles to identify the person you are looking for is also a common practice in Sweden, where variants of the same family name are all grouped together in the directory (Carlson, Carlsohn, Karlson, Karlsohn, will all be found together under Karlsson, the most "official" of the spellings).

Iceland also compels all foreigners seeking Icelandic citizenship to Icelandicize their names (a man whose first name is Lorenz or Lawrence, for instance, has to become Larus, the Icelandic equivalent). Women, who retain their patronymic even after marriage (Maria Hermannsdottir continues to be known by that name even after her marriage to Haraldur Jonsson), are permitted to describe themselves officially as "Mrs." only for purposes of travel abroad.

In a good many Catholic countries, the religious authorities frown upon the bestowing of any name except one appearing in the calendar of saints or in the Scriptures. This means that the appearance of a name not included in either list is prima-facie evidence of free-thinking or atheistic parents. One of Garibaldi's brothers, for instance, bore the first name of Menotti, which was the family name of another Italian freedom fighter. Very recently, the Synod ruling the Greek Orthodox Church instructed its priests to christen children only with the names of saints included in the Orthodox calendar, thereby ruling out such old, classical favorites as Aristotle, Homer, Plato, Socrates and Ulysses. In the Soviet Union, on the other hand, Communist leaders came out with a severe criticism of parents who give their children names which are not Russian in spirit, such as Isolde, Arthur and Ella.

In Brazil, a judge ordered the registrar of births to include the name of Nhyklykrs Wharnes Soures Blel in his records. The parents, living with Indians in central Brazil, insisted this was an Indian name, and the registrar said it was just a jumble of letters. The judge's decision was to the effect that Brazilian parents may call their children anything they want.

A curious custom prevailing in Indonesia is to have no first name at all, but only a family name. This is true of Sukarno, the Indonesian President, and of Soedjatmoko, secretary general of the Indonesian Institute of World Affairs. It is reported, however, that this occasionally leads to confusion among brothers.

The opposite phenomenon often occurs in Britain, where you have a liberal sprinkling of double family names, frequently hyphenated (Coverly-Smith, Scott-Moncrieff, Armstrong-Jones). This is most often done to keep a distinguished name in the maternal line when the other side is not so distinguished, but there are also cases in which adopting a family name about to be extinguished is made the condition of a financial settlement.

This system, occasional in English-speaking lands, is generalized in countries of Spanish speech. The Spanish system calls for two names, the first being that of the father's family, the second that of the mother's. They may or may not be connected by *y,* "and." A recent Mexican President bore this combination in his name, which is Adolfo Ruiz Cortines. This double name may occasionally multiply when a family decides to keep on using the names of both father and mother. One case of this ran as follows: Señora María Teresa de la Fuente Parres y Fernández del Rivero Viuda de González. María and

Teresa are her Christian names; one of her male ancestors was named de la Fuente, and married a Señorita
Parres; their children decided to continue using both
names; thus her father's family name became de la
Fuente Parres. Her mother's family, following the same
practice, became Fernández del Rivero. María Teresa at
birth therefore became a de la Fuente Parres y Fernández del Rivero, and when she married a González she
simply added de González to her collection of maiden
names, becoming Viuda de González ("widow of González") when her husband died.

In Turkey, where for centuries there were only personal names, family names are now compulsory. But the
old custom persists to the extent that a man with a name
like Mahmud Kadoglu is seldom known as Mr. Kadoglu,
but almost invariably as Mr. Mahmud.

In India, the enthusiasm for current five-year plans has
led to the bestowal of such names as Vikas ("development"), Yojana ("plan"), Pragati ("progress"), and Koy-
ana, the name of a river where a big development project
is under way. In part, this custom was borrowed from the
Soviet Union, where such names as Tractor Station are
not unknown.

A change of name, whether given or family, is something that goes back to Biblical days, when Abram
became Abraham, Jacob became Israel, and Naomi
("sweet") was changed to Mara ("bitter"). Even today,
traditional Jews change the name of a critically ill member of the family in order to confuse the Angel of Death,
and in a family where many children have been lost, a
new baby is called Alter ("the old one") till after he

grows up and marries. Popes and sovereigns usually change names upon rising to their offices.

The change of name, which is a thoroughly legal process in most countries, is usually designed to make things easier for the changer and those having dealings with him. In this fashion, many immigrants into this country have changed their foreign names into English equivalents. Occasionally the change is designed to avoid confusion in pronunciation, as when the Lougheed brothers, founders of Lockheed Aircraft, became tired of hearing the name pronounced "log-head" and "low-head," and petitioned the courts for a change. Occasionally it is dictated by reasons of economy, as when immigrants from Holland named Van der Veer changed the spelling to Vandever to save two words in cable charges. Occasionally, the courts refuse to honor the request for a change; this happened when a man named Earl Bottomlee was turned down on his plea to change to Aerlygodlet Wileyelectronspirit Leegravity. The judge stated that the proposed name would only be a handicap to him.

One last naming custom is that of devising a character known by his name and his cartoon portrayal to represent a nation, region, city or group. In this class are America's Uncle Sam (known at an earlier period as Uncle Jonathan), Britain's John Bull, and France's Marianne. Occasionally, side by side with this national character, or totally independent of him, there also arises another character, designed to represent the man in the street, the harassed taxpayer, or the downtrodden member of the nation's poorer classes. There is a John Q. Public (or

John Q. Taxpayer) in the United States, usually pictured as wearing a derby and a barrel, having lost even his shirt to the taxing authorities. Germany has a similar character known as Poor Michael. Paddy is the Irishman *par excellence*. In the Philippines, Juan de la Cruz ("John of the Cross") is the typical lowly worker and voter. Cuba has a Liborio who is the typical sugar-cane worker. In medieval France, long before Marianne came into existence, the peasants identified themselves with a mythical Jacques Bonhomme ("James Goodman"), and when they revolted against their feudal lords, their movement took the name of Jacquerie from this imaginary character.

Cities often have their representatives. Father Knickerbocker, for example, stands for New York. In France, a character named Marius is representative of the city of Marseille. In Italy, Rome has Pasquino, Naples has Pulcinella, Milan has Pinotto, Sicily has Nofrio.

For military groups, there is the French *poilu* ("hairy one"), the typical French doughboy of World War I; there is the British Tommy Atkins, the American G. I. Joe. There is even, though most people don't know it, an ideal WAC, called G. I. Minnie. The name is an abbreviation of Minerva, the goddess worn as an emblem by the Women's Army Corps.

CHAPTER TWENTY

Clues to Family Names

As a final summation of our family name survey, we may go back to our detective technique and endeavor to ascertain, by the form a name takes, what the nationality or national origin of the owner may be. This occasionally comes in handy in a practical way.

German names (and this includes Yiddish ones as well) comprise patronymic forms ending in *-sohn* and common endings like *-stein, -berg, -burg, -mann, -er.* The prefix *von* is normally indicative of German origin, and frequently of an aristocratic family.

For Dutch, the most common prefix is *van*, separated from the rest of the name in the original, often connected with it when the name comes to America (Van Brunt, Van Dyck or Vandike, Vandeventer). *Ten* and *de* also appear as prefixes (Ten Eyck, de Grunigen); this *de* is the Dutch definite article meaning "the," not the preposition meaning "of" that appears in the Romance languages.

Scandinavian names (Swedish, Norwegian, Danish, Icelandic) run heavily to patronymics in -son or -sen; but there are in addition the common endings -quist, -rup, -holm, -strom, -dahl, -gren, -by, -tjen.

Irish and Scots Gaelic share the prefix Mc or Mac (the former is preferred for Irish, the latter for Scottish names); this prefix goes back to a root that means "boy" or "young man," appearing also in the Welsh Ap- (originally Map-), and in the English "maid." O' is characteristically Irish. Fitz-, originally of Norman-French derivation, passes into English, then into Irish names.

The great Spanish patronymic ending is -ez, and Portuguese shares it in the form -es (Spanish Núñez, Portuguese Nunes). Spanish names are often preceded by de ("of"), or by del, de la, de los, de las (all meaning "of the"); Portuguese names also may be preceded by de, but "of the" appears in the forms do, da, dos, das. French names often start with Le- or La- ("the"), or with Du-, Des- ("of the"); they may also be preceded by de, d' ("of"). Italian names usually have vowel endings (-a, -o, -i), but a few of them retain an old Latin form in -is, usually with de before the name (de Ritis, de Gubernatis). Di and de ("of") often appear before the name. The article forms Lo, La, Li ("the") often appear at the beginning of Italian names. Rumanian names run largely to the suffix -escu ("pertaining to": Enescu, Antonescu).

In the Slavic division, Russian prefers the patronymic possessive plural ending -ov (-off) or -ev (-eff), which, if the bearer is feminine, changes to -ova, -eva. The ending

-sky is widespread, and changes to *-skaya* in the feminine. The ending *-ich* or *-vich*, changing to *-vna* in the feminine, indicates the name of one's father, inserted between the first and the family name. Bulgarian shares the *-ev* (*-eff*) ending with Russian. Czech also has *-sky* (feminine *-ská*), while Polish has *-ski* in the masculine, *-ska* in the feminine. Other common Czech endings are *-ak*, *-ek*, *-ik*. Polish also has *-wicz*, pronounced exactly like the Russian *-vich*. Ukranian frequently has the ending *-enko*, and the Serbo-Croatian of Yugoslavia uses *-ić* as a family name ending.

Hungarian family names are often marked by an initial *Sz-*, or by a final *-cs*. Finnish names very frequently end in *-en*. Greek has a predominance of endings in *-poulos* and *-polis*, along with patronymics in *-ou* and other forms in *-as*, *-os*, *-is*. Armenian family names often end in *-ian*, Turkish ones in *-oglu*.

True Hebrew and Arabic names are patronymics, marked by *ben* and *ibn*, respectively. Chinese names are invariably of one syllable. Japanese names are normally of two or more syllables, with *-mura* and *-moto* as common endings and *Yama-* often appearing at the beginning.

For first names, it may be remarked that French and German often have feminine names ending in *-e*, for which the Italian, Spanish or Portuguese equivalent would have *-a*. The latter languages favor *-o* as a masculine ending. Japanese feminine first names often end in *-ko*, a form that means "child."

Certain common elements in names are fairly international, at least in the western languages, and assume predictable forms. The English -*bert* of Albert, Robert, etc., which has the same form in French, appears in Italian and Spanish as -*berto*, in German as -*brecht* or -*precht*. The -*olph* of Adolph, Rudolph, will appear as -*olf* in German, -*olphe* in French, -*olfo* in Italian and Spanish. The ending -*mar* of some German names, like Waldemar, appears as -*mir* in the Slavic languages (Vladimir), from which it was originally borrowed.

Keeping these clues in mind, we may occasionally be able to determine the national origin of a person with whom we happen to be conversing, or whose name we read in the news, and this information may be of use when we least expect it.

Part III

THING NAMES

CHAPTER TWENTY-ONE

From Name to Thing

Personal names, both first and family, often bob up in the most unexpected places, among flowers, foods, articles of attire, elements, constellations, even musical instruments and ordinary tools.

Flowers are frequently named after their discoverers, or in honor of some distinguished individual. Whenever this happens, we may be reasonably certain that the flower is one of comparatively recent discovery or creation, for the old, traditional flowers of Europe bear old, traditional names, built on popular imagery, like violet, pansy (originally the French *pensée*, "thought"), buttercup, cowslip, daffodil (or asphodel), bluebell, periwinkle. Note, however, that marigold contains the name of Mary, and that the botanical name of the daffodil, narcissus, goes back to a mythological character much given to self-admiration, while iris is named after the rainbow goddess of the Greeks.

In more recent times we find bougainvillea, named after a French navigator; begonia, bearing the name of Bégon (Michel Bégon, 1638–1710, a French patron of science); dahlia, after Andreas Dahl, a Swedish botanist; camellia, after the Jesuit Josef Kamel; lobelia, after the Flemish botanist Matthias de Lobel; gloxinia, after the German B. P. Gloxin; zinnia, after a professor of medicine at the University of Göttingen named J. G. Zinn; fuchsia, which takes the name of the botanist Leonhard Fuchs; and magnolia, after the Frenchman Pierre Magnol. There is a pink flower called either bitterroot or lewisia, which is the state flower of Montana and takes its second name from Meriwether Lewis of the Lewis and Clark expedition. There is the poinsettia, named after our first ambassador to Mexico, Joel Roberts Poinsett, appointed in 1825 by President Monroe; he found the flower growing in profusion in Mexico, cultivated it, and finally took the seeds home with him to Charleston, S. C., where he planted it in his garden.

Then there are foods that bear the names of persons. Sandwiches were named after the Earl of Sandwich, who could not take time for regular meals away from the gambling table, and had a slice of meat between two slices of bread brought to him to munch while he gambled. Melba toast and chicken Tetrazzini commemorate two famous opera stars. The French delicacy known as *crèpes suzette* is said to have been originated by a Monte Carlo chef for Edward VII of England and named after Suzette, an attractive flower girl whom His Majesty admired. Pralines, the famed New Orleans delicacy, owe their name to Marshal du Plessis-Praslin of France, whose cook invented them in the early seventeenth century. It is interesting in this connection that if you ask for *Pralinen* in Germany, you will get not a confection of sugar and nuts, but a box of chocolate creams. Two names of this kind come to us from Russia. One is Beef Stroganoff, named after a Russian noble family; the other is the Molotoff cocktail of World War II, which is not a cocktail at all, but a bottle of gasoline ignited with a fuse and used against enemy tanks.

One false personal name appearing in a food item is johnnycake, which was in origin a journey cake, a baked corn cake carried by travelers. Since New Englanders scorned to pronounce the *r* in "journey," the name of the cake became "jouney," then "jonne," finally "johnny."

Among articles of attire that owe their names to persons are the jacket, the pants, and the derby hat. The first takes its name from the French Jacques (Jacques Bonhomme was the medieval French John Q. Taxpayer). He wore a short, tight garment called *jaque* after him; *jaquette* was a diminutive form which passed into English. Pants were at first pantaloons, and the name came from a character in the Renaissance Italian comedy whose name was Pantalone, who wore long, baggy pants, and who always got stuck with the bill; it is probable that his name may have been derived from Saint Pantaleone, one of the patron saints of Venice. The term "derby" was at first applied to a famous horse race in England, instituted at Epsom Downs in 1780 by Lord Derby; the type of hat called derby was often worn to the races ("bowler" is another name for it), and the Brown Derby was popularized by Al Smith in the 1928 election campaign. There is also the mackintosh, invented by Charles Macintosh in the last century, and the raglan, named after Lord Raglan, who led the Charge of the Light Brigade in the Crimean War. Knickers represent part of the costume of Father Knickerbocker, a symbol of old New York.

The various branches of science offer many names that come from persons. In chemistry, two of the nine elements heavier than uranium were recently named einsteinium and fermium, honoring two of the founding fathers of atomic energy, Einstein and Fermi. Uranium itself is named after Uranus, one of the mythological gods of the ancients. Mercury commemorates another god, and both ammonia and amido contain the name of Amon, one of the surnames of Jupiter, who was also the sun god of the Egyptians. Nickel was the Germanic name of a god of the mines, later transferred to the devil (the Old Nick), and applied by German miners to the mineral they called *Kupfernickel*, "the devil's copper." Arsenic comes from a Greek word meaning "man" or "male"; ancient Greek painters used it for painting male faces.

In astronomy, mythological and personal names abound. There are constellations and individual stars like Perseus and Cassiopeia, whose names come straight out of Greek legend; there are Arabic names (the Arabs were the greatest astronomers of the Middle Ages) like Algol, "the mischief maker," so called because of its strange changes in brilliancy. There are new asteroids, named by their discoverers, usually with a modern name. Russian astronomers, for instance, named two of three asteroids they had discovered Lomonosova, in honor of a

famous Russian physicist, and Idelsonia, in honor of one
of their astronomers (the third, however, was given the
name of Postrema, Latin for "last"). Argentinian astronomers in the days of Perón christened two of their discov-
eries Shirtless and Fanatic, both in honor of the Shirtless
(*Descamisado*) supporters of the now exiled dictator.

Meteorologists have to reckon with the names of the
winds, which the ancients personified in such forms as
Aeolus and Auster. Today we have such names as kham-
sin, the fifty-day dry wind of Egypt; the westerly datoo
of Gibraltar; the biting buran of Russia and its Adriatic
equivalent, the bora; the chinook of America and the
foehn of Switzerland; the violent williwaw of Alaska; the
gentle matsukaze of Japan; the mild shamal of Mesopo-
tamia; the typhoon, or "great wind" of the China Seas,
and the monsoon, or seasonal rain wind, of the Indian
Ocean. We also have a personification of hurricanes that
is very similar to the practice of the ancients; the Weather
Bureau gives them girls' names like Diane and Carol.

The ampere, the ohm, the volt, the watt, the galvanom-
eter in electricity, all bear the names of scientists. The
daguerreotype, the guillotine and the silhouette contain
the names of their inventors, Daguerre, Guillotin and
Silhouette. A common tool like the monkey wrench represents not a monkey, but the name of its inventor,
Charles Monckey of Brooklyn. Musical instruments such
as the saxophone and the stradivarius (strad for short)
carry the names of their constructors, Antoine Sax and
Antonio Stradivari. A dance like the bolero bears the
name of its Spanish originator. Macadamized roads were
first created by a man named MacAdam.

There are little used types of champagne bottles (four to twenty-four quarts) which bear the names of Biblical characters: Jeroboam, Methuselah, Salmanazar, Balthazar and Nebuchadnezzar. A mosaic contains the name not of Moses, but of the Muses. An arabesque bears a reference to the Arabs, who devised it. A mausoleum commemorates King Mausolus of Caria, whose tomb was one of the seven wonders of the ancient world. Lazaret is from Lazarus, whom Christ raised from the dead. Simony is from Simon the Magician, who traded on people's credulity. A Jezebel is a reminder of a wicked queen of Biblical days. When you use an atlas, you are reminded of the legendary giant who bore the world on his shoulders. If you are in a panic, it is because you have beheld the great god Pan. If you undergo an odyssey, you are following in the footsteps of Odysseus or Ulysses, who wandered for many weary years after the fall of Troy before he found his way back to his home in Ithaca and his faithful wife Penelope. If a congressman or senator launches a philippic against someone, it is a reminder of the impassioned oratory of Demosthenes against the way Philip of Macedon encroached upon the liberties of the Greek city states.

A cicerone is a guide who takes you on a tour and explains the sights you see, but his name is that of the great Cicero in Italian dress. A dunce is one who is not too intelligent; but the appellation comes from the name of Duns Scotus, a medieval philosopher whose lengthy lucubrations bored his contemporaries. A spoonerism (the sort of accidental or deliberate transposition of sounds that appears in "a well-boiled icicle," or "the pies are all occupewed") was first put into vogue by a Reverend William A. Spooner. Mesmerism, more or less synonymous with hypnotism, was popularized by a Viennese physician named F. A. Mesmer. A marionette bears the name of Marion, a popular female puppet.

Personal and family names appear even in such ultramodern products as cigarettes. Chesterfield is the name of an old, aristocratic English family whose most distinguished member was probably Philip Dormer Stanhope, the fourth Earl of Chesterfield, who was both a statesman and an author and lived in the eighteenth century. His name was first bestowed upon a type of sofa, then upon a kind of coat; now it has become a cigarette brand.

CHAPTER TWENTY-TWO

From Name to Quality

In addition to the personal names that appear as or in common nouns, there is an army of adjectives in which a personal name appears in overt or disguised form.

Practically the entire Graeco-Roman Olympus of gods and goddesses has given rise to qualifying words in common use. Jovial, mercurial, martial, saturnine, venereal, aphrodisiacal, erotic, all call up characteristics of Jupiter, Mercury, Mars, Venus, Aphrodite (merely the Greek name of Venus), Eros (Greek name of Cupid, god of love). Protean means "multiform," and goes back to Proteus, a minor sea-god who had the power to change his shape whenever the fancy seized him. Titanic means "giant-like," and goes back to the Titans, primeval giants who waged war against the gods. Even adjectives like opportune and importunate conceal the name of Portunus, god of ports and harbors; opportune is "coming into port," and importunate is "fending you off from the harbor into which you are trying to sail."

Physicians, on graduating from medical school, take the Hippocratic oath, in which they swear to uphold the noble standards of their profession. This goes back to Hippocrates, an ancient Greek physician who was in some ways the founder of that profession (his name, as you may have figured out, meant "horse ruler"). Epicurean means following the philosophy of Epicurus, who held that pleasure is the supreme goal in life.

Adjectives derived from literary authors or characters are many. One speaks of Machiavellian cunning (Machiavelli was a Renaissance Italian statesman whose writings uphold the principles of statecraft without moral scruples). Shavian is pertaining to or in imitation of the writings of George Bernard Shaw. Quixotic means idealistic to the point of foolishness, and comes from the great character of the Spanish writer Cervantes, Don Quixote, the man who forgot that knighthood was no longer in flower and went tilting against the windmills, since he could find no giants to oppose him. Gargantuan comes from one of the characters of the French writer Rabelais, a sort of fictional Superman. Pickwickian is often said of people or situations that remind one of Dickens' *Pickwick Papers.* The Russians, going English speakers one better on America's own preserves, have devised a literary adjective that we lack, *marktvenovsky,* "pertaining to or like Mark Twain," who is probably the favorite American writer in Russia.

In the field of science, adjectives from personal names abound, but that is rather natural, since here the tendency would be to name things after their discoverers. Malpighi, an Italian anatomist of the seventeenth century, has thus given his name to Malpighian corpuscles, layers and tubes; and the Eustachian tubes, forming part of the human ear, bear the name of Eustachio, an Italian physician of the sixteenth century. An adjective like chauvinistic, meaning "nationalistic to an excessive degree," reflects the name of Nicolas Chauvin, a soldier of Napoleon, whose demonstrations of patriotism were such as to arouse the ridicule even of his comrades.

Two adjectives in which a personal name lies deeply hidden are tawdry and maudlin. The first is a contraction of Saint Audrey, at whose fair in medieval England cheap, shoddy objects were sold. The other goes back to Magdalen, because Mary Magdalen was often depicted dishevelled and with eyes red from weeping.

In addition to the adjectives, there are the verbs that bear someone's name. Tantalize goes back to Tantalus, a mythological character who was punished for his crimes by being chained just out of reach of food and drink. Vulcanize is a modern term, but draws its name from Vulcan, the Roman fire-god. When we speak of hectoring someone, we mean "to bully or persecute"; Hector was the Trojan leader who wrought havoc among the Greeks in the absence of his archadversary Achilles, who finally came back to the scene of the fighting and slew him. To out-Herod someone means "to outdo him in violence," and the reference is to the massacre of the innocents ordered by King Herod.

To bowdlerize is to apply a type of literary censorship that was applied to the works of Shakespeare by a man named Bowdler at the outset of the 19th century. During World War I, to hooverize meant to save food, in accordance with the urging of Herbert Hoover, then Food Administrator.

Modern civilization has given us such verbs as to pasteurize, which means to put milk through a germ-killing process first devised by Louis Pasteur; to Sanforize, which is to put material through a process that prevents shrinking; even to Fletcherize, a term that was popular some decades ago, and meant to chew your food a certain number of times before swallowing it, in accordance with the prescription of an American author named Horace Fletcher. One of the very latest verbs in this field is to Martinize, which is to put clothes through a process claimed to be superior to ordinary dry cleaning.

CHAPTER TWENTY-THREE

Animal Names

Animals, being animate and mobile, come rather close to the human being, and when they are definitely known, as is the case with household pets and race horses, seem to call for something more in the way of a name than just the generic "cat," "cow," "horse" and "chicken," or even the generalized pet name of the type of Pussy, Bossie, Dobbin and Biddy.

To begin with, however, it may be well to remind the reader that there are several names of animal species which contain a human name. Jackdaw has the name of Jack, rabbit that of Robert, magpie that of Mag or Margaret, and both parrot and petrel involve Peter. Ladybug is "the bug of Our Lady."

The word "maverick" as applied to cattle—it can be either a noun or an adjective—is derived from the Maverick family name, well known in Texas. A maverick is

an unbranded steer, hence a nonconformist, and Western
legend had it that at ranch roundups any unclaimed
calves were given the Maverick brand. In his book
A *Maverick American* the late Maury Maverick, author
and member of Congress, explained that although his
grandfather Samuel Augustus Maverick did give the
name to cattle, he was never a rancher or a cattleman, but
once acquired a herd of cattle in payment of a debt.
Until they could be sold the cattle were kept safely on a
peninsula, from which they could not stray, so needed no
branding. But people en route to the '49 gold rush
"talked a great deal about Maverick's cattle that were
never branded" and the name stuck.

Fictional personification of animals encourages the bestowal of names. Bre'r Rabbit is rather modern, but his
origins are lost in the mists of antiquity. The older leg-
ends have Bruin the Bear, Reynard the Fox, Chantecler
the Rooster, Isegrim the Wolf, and many others, whose
names go back to picturesque concepts (Bruin is "the
brown one," Reynard is, sarcastically, "the pure in heart,"
Chantecler is "the clear singer"). But all this is symbolical
and legendary.

Pet names for household animals are really in the nature of first names. Fido, one of the traditional names for
dogs, goes back to the same root that gives us "faith,"
"fidelity" and "federation." Such dog names as Brownie,
Blackie, Buddy, Lucky, are self-explanatory, and are of
the descriptive type. There are also, of course, the fancy
names that are inflicted upon pedigreed hounds. One
Pekinese bore the resounding name of Pinky Pankie Poo,
and others, particularly if they are Dobermans, Weimar-

aners, or other specialized German breeds, bear names reminiscent of the Prussian aristocracy, with *von* and *zu* thrown in.

When it comes to cats, there is at least as much choice. One book of pet names suggests Jumbo for a large specimen (Jumbo, however, seems better reserved for elephants), Smidgen and Trinket for small ones, Tar Baby and Black Witch for color, Fluffy, Pop-Eye and Squeaky for other traits, along with Blitz, Pokey, Spunky and Prissy.

The choices of a famous cat expert include such names as Bee-Bop, Bozo, Canasta, Doxy Faux Pas, Hokum, Sassafras, Voodoo, Wonderboy and Zipper, with humorous forms like Schnoozlefritz and Dinkadoo, and a whole series of twin names: Willy and Nilly, Grin and Bearit, Skin and Bones, Dilly and Dally, Hi and Mitey, Hue and Cry, Rise and Shine. Chumplet, Honey Chile, Wet Smack and Jealousy Pie have also been recorded.

A special problem arises with Siamese cats, who call for Siamese (Thai) names. Here some recommendations are: Mali ("jasmine"), Nam Phueng ("honey"), Chanthra ("moon"), Kla ("brave"), Sakda ("famous for battle"), Satra ("weapon"), Som Phong ("chip off the old block"), Mana ("persistence"), Thong Kon ("gold lump"), Bun Ma ("lucky"). There are even a couple of Siamese pet names that have an English meaning, although a different one: Sap ("wealth") and Sin ("money"). And there are the pseudo-Oriental names, such as Pitti Sing and Me Too.

The names bestowed upon racing horses are more than a luxury; they are a necessity, since the horses have to be precisely identified for racing purposes. Man-o'-War and Upset, who beat him, are quite famous. Less known are Easy Day, Shut Out, Sand Lot, Columbus Day (one of his parents was Discovery, the other was Easy Day, and the ideas were combined). The children of Delicacy and Questionnaire were named Hash, Monday Lunch and Picnic. One horse line blended Chance Shot and Kinswoman to produce Hasty Wedding, and then went on to Gretna Green and Swing-and-Sway. From the line of Shut Out (his owner was evidently a baseball fan) came One-Hitter, Night Game, Ball Hawk, and Three-and-Two.

In the medieval French epic poems, not only every horse, but every sword bears a name. Roland, whose last stand at Roncevaux antedated Custer's exploit by about a thousand years, had a horse named Veillantif ("wakeful") and a sword called Durendal ("hard or enduring"). Tachebrun ("brown spot") and Hauteclaire ("high-clear") are the names of another famous horse and another famous sword in the same poem. Don Quixote's nag in Cervantes' parody of the knightly romance is Rosinante, a name derived from the Spanish word for "nag," which is connected with our own word "horse." So the Silvers of our day have had their precursors.

The naming process is carried on by some Americans to include even the family automobile. One battered old jalopy I have known bore the name of Rosie; another one had the more resounding title of Suzabella.

CHAPTER TWENTY-FOUR

Trade Names

The firm name is a relatively modern product, though we have record in antiquity of producers of certain articles inscribing their names on the products themselves (the oldest document of Latin is a belt buckle which bears the inscription "Manius made me for Numasius," thus indicating both producer and consumer). But this can hardly be described as a firm name of the type of Merrill, Lynch, Pearce, Fenner and Smith, which indicates that people bearing those names are engaged in a certain line of activity.

The firm name, as a rule, simply includes the personal names of the principals engaged in the business. The trade name is subtly different. It may or may not include either a personal name or the name of a product. Often it is simply a catchword, designed to seize the consumer's fancy.

Smith Brothers cough drops, Edison electric appliances, Winchester rifles, Stetson hats, Goodrich tires, are samples of trade names involving a personal name, either that of a founder or that of a discoverer or inventor. They are seldom eye catching, though they may be quite well known. But they sometimes pass from the field of specific trade names to that of ordinary common nouns, as happened to an article of attire known as bloomers, which bear the name of Mrs. Amelia Bloomer, who first advocated the costume. William Ewart Gladstone, Queen Victoria's Prime Minister, is rightly or wrongly said to have given his name to the Gladstone type of carriage, the Gladstone bag, and even the Gladstone wine.

The name of an original inventor or manufacturer sometimes passes into the common domain, so that the article becomes universally known by that name, even if made by someone else. This is the case with Wedgwood china, first devised and produced by Josiah Wedgwood in the eighteenth century, now produced by a number of firms. In most countries of Europe and Latin America, any safety razor is known as a Gillette, though the name should be applied only to the type of product manufactured by the company that bears the name.

Attention may be called at this point to the gradual shift in trade names of the Gillette or Ford type, connected with the inventor or rugged individualist founding the business, to the type of name now dreamed up by ad agencies for corporation products. In the Ann Page products sold by A & P stores, the initials make a tie-in with the grocery chain. There are also a number of artificially personalized products, such as the Betty Crocker line, the Mary Kitchen hash made by Hormel, and others of the same type, where the name is chosen to suggest the sort of thing "Mother used to make."

The picturesque, eye-and-ear catching type of trade name, however, is seldom one that contains a personal name, though it may occasionally contain a slang term, like "Two Guys from Harrison Supermarkets." Far more often it is a word applied by accident or design, like Ivory (soap), Walkover (shoe), Greyhound (bus), all products of someone's fancy; or, better yet, generic words like aspirin, cellophane, victrola, kodak, or Coke (the last is a popular abbreviated form of Coca-Cola).

One of the earliest applications of trade names was to wines. These are generally known by the name of the region that produces them (Champagne, Burgundy, Chianti), but often another element enters into the composition of the name, designed to tell the type or the condition of the grape harvest. French champagnes will often bear the designation *sec* or *brut* or *demi-sec*, indicating degree of dryness, and German wines may bear forms like *Auslese, Spätlese, Beerenauslese* and *Trockenbeerenauslese*, indicating at what point of ripeness the grapes have been picked. Popular distortion sometimes leads to strange results, as in the case of bock beer, which originally was produced in the Hanover town of Einbeck, and was dialectally known as Ainpock ("from Einbeck"); this became corrupted to *ein Bock*, because it sounded like the German words for "a goat." Today, the goat is a symbol for bock beer.

Nowhere does the creation of trade names take such extensive form as in science, where machines like Univac and products like Sulfabenzydrine are turned out by the thousands and have to be given specific names. One dictionary produced by a large drug company consists of nearly two hundred pages and lists the names of 42,000 of the firm's synthetic creations. The strangest part of this is that the dictionary has not been compiled by human beings, but by a machine supplied by International Business Machines. The machine was set to work turning out names that had to be easy to pronounce, spell, remember, translate into foreign languages, and sound medically plausible. On the basis of the indication that suitable drug names like Terramycin and Tetracyn are composed of a two-syllable prefix and a one- or two-syllable ending, the machine went to work, and in less than two hours supplied the firm with thousands of new names for its products, names of the type of Abechamycin, Byulamycin, Platuphyl, Cliohacyn, and Starycide.

One form of trade name which has recently enjoyed vast popularity is that bestowed upon a fair or exposition with the ending -orama appended (the prototype of this ending is panorama, a combination of the Greek pan, "all," and orao, "to see," which means a complete or comprehensive view). Formed in this fashion, we have "contemporama" (a view of what goes on at present), "centorama" (a view of a centennial celebration), and even "Southorama" (an exhibition of products and industries of the South) and "Africanorama" (a similar view of Africa).

Leading among trade names are those bestowed upon transportation lines and even individual trains, railroad cars, ships and planes. The ships, of course, came first, since they existed in antiquity, while the other forms of transportation did not. Among names of steamship lines that arouse visions of far-flung regions of the earth are the Buccaneer Line, the Clipper Line, the British and German Lloyds, and the Japanese Kaishas. Railroad lines are, as a rule, prosaically named, though their trains are not. These include, among others, the famed Orient Express from Paris to Istanbul, and, in America, such attractive names as the Phoebe Snow, the Trail-Blazer, the Red Arrow, the Golden Triangle, the Cavalier, the Connecticut Yankee and the Twentieth Century.

To go into the names of the good ships that have sailed the seven seas since the days of the Phoenicians and the Cretans and the Quest of the Golden Fleece would be a task calling for a separate volume. Columbus' *Niña*, *Pinta* and *Santa María*, Hudson's *Half Moon*, the *Independence*, *Ile de France*, *Queen Mary*, *Conte Biancamano*, and countless other ships are fairly indicative of the naming process that goes into the vessels that ply the world's waters. *Experiment* was the name of the first American ship that sailed directly from the United States to China; the 80-ton sloop left its home port of Albany, N.Y., in 1785, and returned from Canton in 1787. The ceremony of christening two new ships, the *Halliburton 209* and the *Halliburton 210*, was conducted recently in New Orleans in two unfamiliar tongues, designed to honor, as were the ships themselves, the cities of New Orleans and Duncan, Oklahoma. In French and in the tongue of the Oklahoma Indians, the christening formula sounded like this: "Je te baptise Halliburton deux cent neuf" and "Ilappa chi hochifoli Halliburton talepa tuklo acucha pololi."

Names of air lines include not only the familiar American ones, but also the picturesque French *Air France*, the Belgian *Sabena*, the Australian *Qantas*, the Israeli *El Al*, the abbreviated British BOAC, Italian LAI and Dutch KLM. There is Indo-China's *Domaine Agricole de l'Ouest*, New Zealand's *Rural Aviation Ltd.*, Finland's *Rajavartiostojen Esikunta*, Colombia's *Avianca*, Germany's *Lufthansa* and Spain's *Iberia*.

Types of commercial planes are sometimes named, like the British Constellation jets. Military types almost invariably are. The French are perhaps the most imaginative name creators in this field. *Mystère* ("mystery") is the name of one of their best fighting planes, while two types of helicopters are known as *Alouette* ("lark") and *Djinn*. We have our Hellcats, Flying Fortresses and Saber Jets. During World War II we invented our own designations, like Betty and Zero, for some of the enemy's planes. At the present time, we have devised a whole series of full-fledged "pet" names for what the Russians abbreviate into Yak, Mig and La; we call them, according to their types, Fin, Fritz, Fang, Flora, Fagot (all names beginning with F) if they are fighters; Bulls, Beagles, Bisons and Badgers (all names beginning with B) if they are bombers.

Titles of movies are, in a sense, trade names, since upon them the success of the picture often depends. One extremely curious title, which at least could not be easily lost in the shuffle, was "Phffft." One reviewer remarked at the time that now we might expect to have a rash of movies titled "Z-Z-Z-Z-Z" or, better yet, "Son of Z-Z-Z-Z-Z," along with "Ugh," "HM-m-m," "Whew," and "Ho Hum"; but this has not yet materialized.

One final field in which the trade name has arrived is that of haircuts. Taking their cue, perhaps, from the very picturesque names of perfumes on the market, the barbers went to work and devised the following names for special types of haircuts: Fatale, Mohawk Pomp, Pigeon-Breasted Back, Foam Swirl, Fountain Head, U-Turn Swirl, Elvis, Caesar, Tiara-Boom D. A., Madison Avenue, Feather Crew, and Butch. These now take their place with the old, staid, conservative Crew Cut. Two of them, it will be noted, are derived from personal names.

CHAPTER TWENTY-FIVE

Institutional Names

Typical of institutions and their multiform names are our private colleges and universities. Here the naming process follows the customary forms, with the institutions being named after their founders or other prominent people; on the basis of their geographical location; or with descriptive names.

The first type of name predominates in the East and South, the second in the Midwest and West. Such famous names as Yale and Harvard commemorate early founders, while people who have provided the bulk of the endowment appear in names like Carnegie and Duke. Names of famous persons go back in history to Albertus Magnus and Gustavus Adolfus, then come forward in time to William and Mary, George Washington, Lewis and Clark, Humboldt, Sam Houston, Brandeis. The South, far more than the North, specializes in names that include both the first and the second name of the person the college honors. There is a Bessie Tift College in Georgia, a Flora MacDonald in North Carolina, a George Peabody in Tennessee, a Philander Smith in Arkansas, a Bob (not Robert) Jones in South Carolina, even a Mary Hardin Baylor in Texas. The North's Sarah Lawrence, on the other hand, is definitely in the minority. Foreign localities and universities are commemorated in Heidelberg (Ohio), Upsala (New Jersey), Viterbo (Wisconsin), Transylvania (Kentucky). A city of classical antiquity appears in Tusculum (Tennessee).

Religious names abound, with a Jewish Yeshiva, Protestant Wesleyans, Friends Universities and Southern Methodists, Catholic Sacred Hearts, Notre Dames and numerous saints (Saint John is perhaps the one of most frequent occurrence), along with family names of church leaders most of whom were saints (Loyola, Gonzaga).

Poetry appears in such names of colleges as The Citadel, in South Carolina, and the College of the Sequoias, in California, with Bryn Mawr, Cymric for "Big Hill," disguising its poetry under foreign dress. Adelphi contains the same brotherly root as Philadelphia. Principles of one sort or another appear in Alliance College, Defiance College, Principia College (the last is in Illinois). A little confusion appears, too. There are far too many Washingtons and George Washingtons for comfort. Miami University is in Ohio, not in Florida, though there is also a University of Miami at Coral Gables in Florida (interestingly, these two Miamis are completely unrelated, coming from two entirely different words in two different Indian languages). There is a Dickinson College in Carlisle, Pa., and a Fairleigh Dickinson University in Rutherford, N. J. Columbia University in New York used to be known as King's College; that title is now borne by an institution of higher learning in Wilkes-Barre, Pa. Among names that arouse mild curiosity are Beaver College, in Jenkintown, Pa., and Dropsie College in Philadelphia. There is even an altogether mythical institution known as Old Siwash, symbolical of college spirit and alumni reunions.

Geographical names range all the way from compass designations (Northwestern, Southeastern) to plain names of states and cities (University of Nebraska, New York University).

Newspapers, like colleges and universities, are institutions of information and occasionally learning. Here the general run of names covers such designations as Times, Tribune, Gazette, Dispatch, Journal, Post, Inquirer, Examiner, and similar words indicative of the newspaper's function. These are frequently combined and blended as newspapers merge, so that we have, to take our examples from New York alone, a Herald-Tribune, a Journal-American and a World-Telegram and Sun. Political designation (Democrat or Republican) often appears in or out of combination.

In addition to these run-of-the-mill titles, there are plenty of unusual ones that display the name-forming ingenuity of their founders. There is, for instance, a Woodbine (Iowa) Twiner, a Linn (Missouri) Unterrified Democrat, a Tombstone (Arizona) Epitaph, a Ferris (Texas) Wheel. Walnut Creek, Cal., has its Walnut Kernel; Oilton (Okla.) has its Gusher; Yellville (Ark.) has its Echo; and North East (Pa.) has its Breeze.

Other interesting names in the newspaper world include Avalanche, Tornado, Rough Notes, Eccentric, Joker, Play Spots. There is unalloyed frankness in such names as Facts and Fallacies, and Agitator. New Orleans' Times-Picayune is rivalled by Jefferson's (Texas) Jimplecute. There is even a journal called Mosquito News published in New Jersey, which sounds like a complete giveaway for that state.

Radio and TV have blossomed forth into institutions of information rivalling both newspapers and colleges. Here the names tend to be noncommittal, consisting simply of letters. But the letters can be arranged in such a way as to produce an effect, as proved by stations KOLD and KOOL, both in Arizona, WARM, in Scranton, WELL, in Battle Creek. There is KORN in Mitchell, S. D., KAKE in Wichita, KATL in Miles City, Montana, and KOAL in Price, Utah. KOME is in Tulsa, but WENT is in Gloversville, N.Y. There is a WOOF in Alabama, a WREN in Topeka, a CROW in Oakland. You'll find WORK in York, Pa., KASH in Eugene, and KOIN in Portland, Oregon. WHO is in Des Moines, but its objective case WHOM is in New York. The home city is honored in KSOO, Sioux Falls, but foreign localities seem to be mentioned in KUBA, Yuba, and KIEV, Glendale, Cal.

Occasionally a station's letters spell out the initials of a person whom it is wished to honor. Thus, New York's WEVD bears the initials of Eugene V. Debs, an old-line Socialist leader. Occasionally peculiar effects result from the meaning of a station's call letters in a foreign language; this happened when the Voice of America beamed its messages to the Soviet Union over Station WRUL; the first three letters come close enough to the Russian *vru*, "I am lying," to cause belly laughs in the Kremlin.

CHAPTER TWENTY-SIX

National Group Names

We saw in connection with place names that there is often an intimate connection between the land and the group that occupies it. The link is a two-way one, and frequently reverses itself. A tribe or group may call itself by a certain name, give this name to the land, then take it back in the form of a national or regional name for the inhabitants. It is often as idle to speculate about which came first, the group name or the place name, as it is to wonder about the priority of the chicken or the egg.

There is, however, one thing to be said. In a large number of cases the group name remains such, and does not give rise to a place name, save in such vague forms as The Land of the Iroquois, or The Country of the Sioux. This is particularly true in the case of cultures discovered in relatively recent times, as with our own American Indians, and perhaps affords a clue as to the priority of group or place names.

Even in antiquity, we find a certain number of tribal group names that either have no place name corresponding to them, or definitely gave rise to the place name. The city of Paris undoubtedly owes its name to the tribe of the Parisii, not the other way around. On the other hand, we find such group names as Pelasgians, an ancient Mediterranean race, the root of which is a word meaning "wide and flat" ("placid," "please" and "placate" are among the common words derived from the same root); here the group name would seem to mean "flat-landers," so in a sense it might be said the description of the region led to the name of the group. Another ancient root, meaning "to bristle or prickle," appears in the place name Chersonese (now Kherson, coinciding more or less with the Soviet Union's Crimea), and in the name of the old Italic tribe of the Hirpini ("hirsute" or "hairy"); here application of the root to the name of the group would seem to precede its application to a locality. Hyperborean comes from a root meaning "mountain" (it appears also in aurora borealis); here the locality comes first. Lapland gets its name from its inhabitants, the Lapps, and their name seems to go back to a Swedish designation meaning "blockheads" (the root word means "lip"). Another clear case where the group name not only comes first, but is unaccompanied by a place name is that of the Samoyeds, a tribe of Siberia; here the name was bestowed by the Russians, and means "self-eating," or "cannibal."

American Indian tribes often bear names that are neither derived from place names nor give rise to such. The Apaches of the Southwest, for instance, get their name from the Zuñi *apachu*, meaning "enemy"; the Sem-

inoles go back to Creek Indian *asi-yohola* that means
"black drink," evidently a reference to the swamps of the
Everglades; the name of the Navajos means "great fields,"
or "great plains." The Bantu tribes of southern Africa
bear a collective name meaning "people" or "men," but
it was inflicted upon them by a white man. In like manner, the Kaffirs have an Arabic name meaning "infidel."

The national names of the inhabitants of most modern
nations are of modern formation, and depend upon the
place name. The Romans were the inhabitants of Rome,
just as their descendants the Italians are the inhabitants
of Italy, and Americans the inhabitants of America. In
many cases, the regular national name has given rise to
secondary names which may be self-bestowed, in which
case they are often complimentary, or bestowed by
others, and then may range from noncommittal to insult-
ing. But they may also spectacularly change their connotation. There is the case of the American Yankee,
concerning whose origin there is so much doubt. Is it
really an Indian mispronunciation of "English"? Is it derived from a Cherokee word meaning "coward" or
"slave," bestowed by the Virginians upon the New Englanders for refusing to help them against the Indians,
and later, after Bunker Hill and Lexington, turning into
a title of glory (at least for the North; troops from the
South were quite angry at being called Yanks by Euro-
peans in the two World Wars)? Or is it one of a dozen
other things claimed by various experts? The French inhabitants of Quebec call themselves Habitants, "inhabitants" *par excellence.* Those people of French origin
whom the British deported to Louisiana as described in

Longfellow's *Evangeline* still glory in the designation of Cajun, which is a corruption of Acadien or Acadian (Acadia was the name of the French Canadian settlement).

Typical of uncomplimentary group designations are Mex, bestowed by Texans upon people of Mexican origin in their midst; or the Polack resented by people of Polish ancestry, though it comes closer to their own designation for themselves than either Pole or Polish; or Bohunk, said to be a cross between Bohemian and Hungarian, applied indiscriminately to people from the former Hapsburg Empire; or the Pommie and Geordie applied by Australians to newly arrived immigrants from England and Scotland. There are regional group names, often of obscure origin, applied in uncomplimentary fashion by the people of one section of a country to those of another, like Damyank and Cracker in the United States; or Maragatos, which southern Spaniards use for the Galicians and Leonese of northern Spain, or Cafoni, applied by northern to southern Italians (for Maragatos, no satisfactory explanation is available, despite the "cat" ending of the word; Cafoni is said to have originated with a Roman centurion by the name of Cafo, living in the days of Cicero, but this is quite doubtful). With a great many of the above terms, it is optional with the recipient whether he wants to treat the word as a joke or as an insult.

A secondary distortion of group names appears in modern newspaper headlines, where we have such abbreviated forms as Yugos, Balts, Liths, Bulgars, Serbs, for Yugoslavs, Baltic peoples, Lithuanians, Bulgarians,

Serbians, or downright historical anachronisms, like Norse for Norwegians.

Asian has replaced the Asiatic of our youth, and for this various reasons are alleged: one is that the ending of Asian coordinates with that of European, African, American; another, very doubtful, one is that Asiatic is offensive, having been used in offensive connotations in the past (note, however, that the ending appears in such words as "Hanseatic" and "numismatic").

Many groups have come to glory in a designation originally intended to be a term of derision coined by their opponents. This is true of Whig and Tory, of Methodist and Quaker, of Yankee (if we accept one of the accounts given above); even of Cowboy, a term first applied to the Tory guerrillas who, during the Revolution, fought for George III in what is now Westchester County, N.Y., and later revived by Ewen Cameron and his riders after Texas had won its independence from Mexico.

The terms American and Yankee recently came in for serious misunderstanding in Pakistan and Iran. In the former country, tribesmen requested the government officials to let them meet and thank the Amir Khan ("rich landlord") who had been making them gifts of wheat. The wheat, it was finally explained to them, was not from any Amir Khan, but was of Am-er-i-can origin, from the people of a country far away across the sea. The Iranians, on the other hand, took to Yankee with a vim, only pronounced it Yengueh, a contraction of Yengueh Donyai, which means "New World people" in Iranian; not at all a bad name for the Yankees.

CHAPTER TWENTY-SEVEN

Other Group Names

As an honorary and honorable sample of names of smaller groups, we may take the popular names of some American baseball teams. These really belong to the nickname class, as shown by the Dodgers, once called the Brooklyn Trolley Dodgers, and at various times known by other designations, such as Bridegrooms, Superbas, and Bums; or the Braves, formerly known as the Red Stockings, Doves, Redcaps and Beaneaters. The Giants got their name from one of their managers back in 1885; after looking over the array, he blurted out: "These blokes are giants!", and the name stuck.

Phillies is a geographical designation; a contest was at one time run to devise another name for them, and the winning entry was Bluejays, but the name never took. Orioles, on the other hand, did for the Baltimore team; but that is because there is actually a Baltimore oriole.

In like manner, the Chicago White Stockings turned into the Colts, on account of their friskiness; then into the Orphans, because of the lack of a ball park; lastly, because of their bearlike strength and playful disposition, they became the Cubs.

Red Stockings, Reds and Redlegs have at various times described the Cincinnati team. The Pittsburgh Pirates were so named because they raided other clubs for talent when first formed in 1887. The Boston Red Sox came up from a series of titles that included Somersets, Puritans, Plymouth Rocks and Speed Boys. St. Louis changed its color designation from Browns to Maroons to Cardinals. The Detroit Tigers owe their name to the black and yellow striped hose they once wore. Senators is an obvious name for a Washington team; Athletics is descriptive; and Yankees, which would seem at first blush to be a name for a New England group, was bestowed in anger by a press writer who found the old name of Highlanders too long for the headlines.

Other legitimate group names include those of military forces, some of which are generic, like the French *poilu*, the British Tommy Atkins, England's military man since time immemorial, and the American Doughboy, later known as G. I. Joe. The Anzacs were the Australia–New Zealand Army Corps, and the name was made up of the initials. But the New Zealanders were also known as Kiwis, from the Maori name of an almost extinct flightless bird found only in New Zealand. The South Africans called their soldiers Springboks, after one of the numerous gazelles of the region. Then there are group names of individual units, like Devil Dogs, or Leathernecks,

applied to the U. S. Marines, the Blue Devils, applied to
the French Chasseurs des Alpes, the Scarponi ("Big
Shoes"), applied to the Italian Alpine troops. Smaller individual units, too, had their special designations, like
Baron von Richthofen's Knights of the Flying Circle of
the early German Air Force, the Death's Head Hussars
of the Prussian Army, and, long before them, the Polish
Winged Hussars of Jan Sobieski, who saved Vienna from
the encircling Turks, and the Flying Tigers of World
War II.

The transition from the military to the criminal is supplied by the common element of violence. It is sometimes
difficult to tell where one ends and the other begins.
Among the most famous blends of military and criminal
group names of the past is one that has given rise to a
synonym for "murderer," Assassin. This is the Arabic
Hashishin, those who drug themselves with hashish in
order to commit deeds of violence. The sect was founded
in the eleventh century by a Persian preacher, Hasan
Sabbah, who, opposing the ruling monarch, seized a
mountain fortress and there organized his fanatical
horde, which later operated against the Crusaders. Another name for the sect was *Fida'is*, or "self-sacrificers."
Methods similar to theirs, though without benefit of the
drug, were later employed by the Spanish guerrillas and
Lützow's German Night Riders in the Napoleonic Wars,
by the French *Franc Tireurs* ("free shooters") in the
Franco-Prussian War of 1870, by the Partisans and
Maquis of the Underground movements in World War
II (*Maquis*, by the way, means "underbrush," and refers to the dense thickets of Corsica, which used to

shelter bandits of the Robin Hood type). The Nihilists
of Czarist Russia were revolutionary groups dedicated to
overthrowing the existing regime. The Sinn Fein ("ourselves alone") groups of Ireland, which later turned into
the Irish Republican Army, or I.R.A., were similarly
dedicated to getting the British out of their country.
Haganah ("the defense") and Irgun zvai Leumi ("organization for the people") were the names of two Hebrew
semimilitary groups that contributed to the creation of
the State of Israel. In still more recent times, we have had
the Mau Mau ("hidden ones") of Kenya, an organization
of Kikuyu tribesmen vowed to destroy the white man's
rule in East Africa.

There is a point at which military action, even of the
underground type, fades and purely criminal action begins, and here we have names of organizations and gangs
galore. Mafia and Camorra were (and possibly are) two
criminal groups, one Sicilian, the other Neapolitan,
founded originally on the Robin Hood or resistance principle against feudal injustice, later degenerating into
groups of terrorists and blackmailers pure and simple.

One famous criminal group of America in the last century was the Molly Maguires, a band of Pennsylvania
anthracite-region terrorists whose violence stirred the
nation in the 1870's. The gang's power was broken with
the conviction and hanging of twenty Molly Maguires
between 1877 and 1879. They had been antedated by
organizations known as the Hearts of Steel and the
Hearts of Oak, formed against the landowners of Ireland.

Purely criminal gangs in America prior to the Civil

War produced such group names as the True Blue Americans, the Atlantic Guard, and the Dead Rabbits, who seem to have been the first to employ women in battle. Whyos, Little Augies and the Purple Gang came after these.

CHAPTER TWENTY-EIGHT

Abbreviated Names

There is one type of abbreviation which is a mere contraction, like the headline Chisox for Chicago Sox. The other, and more widespread, type is the use of capitalized initials for names consisting of two or more words. In this class we find even names of nations, like U.S.S.R. for Union of Socialist Soviet Republics, U.K. for United Kingdom, and U.S.A., which serves both the United States of America and the Union of South Africa.

Railway, air and steamship lines often abbreviate their names in one or the other fashion. We have familiar, affectionate contractions like Pennsy for Pennsylvania Railroad, Chessie for Chesapeake and Ohio (but also, more officially, C. & O.), and then a whole rash of initials, like B. & O. for Baltimore and Ohio, D. L. & W. for Delaware, Lackawanna and Western, B. & M. for Boston and Maine. The American air line TWA, the British BOAC, the Italian LAI, the Dutch KLM, are all of this type, and many people using them are totally ignorant of their full names.

In the field of business and industry, we find corporate persons often known almost entirely by their initials. Who cares to speak of International Business Machines, General Motors, Metro-Goldwyn-Mayer, when I.B.M., G.M. and M.G.M. are available? Or, going a little beyond initials, is not Alcoa a perfect substitute for Aluminum Company of America, and Nabisco for National Biscuit Company? There are even such slogans as Uneeda (Biscuit).

In addition to the popular abbreviations, there are the technical ones that appear on the Stock Exchange, where brevity is of the essence. Here every stock listed has a letter abbreviation by which it is designated for trading purposes. Some of the abbreviations are one letter (A for Anaconda Copper, T for American Tel. & Tel.); but of these there are only 22, with I, O, W and Q not utilized; Q is reserved for bankrupt firms, and is placed before the normal symbol when they get into trouble. The letter designations are usually the initials or first letters of the firm name, like JM for Johns Manville, or ARG for Argo Oil, but since the alphabet has its limitations, you will also find some arbitrary symbols, like V for the New Haven Railroad and Z for Woolworth, or symbols that are in part arbitrary, like KSU for Kansas City Southern Railway and TV for Tidewater Oil. At any rate, the Exchange assures us that the tape will never spell out MUD, DIP or BUM.

Some of these letter abbreviations give rise to nicknames. NP for Northern Pacific becomes "Nipper" among the stock brokers. BS for Bethlehem Steel turns into "Bessy," while NV for North American Aviation comes out as "Navy."

In the manufacturing field, alphabetic abbreviations are normally avoided because of the publicity value of a full, resounding trade name. Still, we have one glaring case where the initials of a firm ultimately led to the generic name of the product, whether manufactured by them or by other firms. This is B.V.D., which originally stood for Bradley, Voorhis & Day, manufacturers of men's undergarments.

The British, a little less given to abbreviations than we, at least in the field of business (note their M.P. for Member of Parliament and V.C. for one who has received the Victoria Cross, one of the highest military honors in the land), nevertheless are succumbing to the desire for brevity. One of their most time-honored banking firms, Barclays Bank (Dominion, Colonial and Overseas) recently changed to Barclays Bank D. C. O. The bank officials stated that the change had been made "in the interests of efficiency and economy, and to avoid the difficulties connected with the translation of the name into other languages."

The Russians, whose language tends to run to long words anyhow, make use of alphabetic abbreviations to an even greater extent than we do. GUM, for instance, is the name you will find over their big Moscow department store. It stands for *Gosudarstvenny Universalny Magazin*, or "Government Universal Store."

Letter abbreviations of government bureaus have been

notorious since the days of confusion between WPA, PWA, etc. The longest alphabetical agency name on record is said to be JDODAGSAIACODOSAPP, which stands for "Joint Department of Defense and General Services Administration Industry Advisory Committee on Disposal of Surplus and Personal Property."

Science offers its own needed abbreviations, which are a must if a layman (or even a scientist) is to utter the names of certain compounds. Anyone can say D.D.T., but even chemists would have trouble with Dichloro-diphenyltrichloroethane, which destroys moths and other insects. Mono–D.N.C.H.P. may sound bad, but the original name for a product that kills the mites of moths sounds worse: Monoethanolamine-dinitrocyclohexyl-phenolate.

The Navy has found it desirable to abbreviate the designations of the various types of vessels (about two hundred of them) that comprise a modern fleet. Here we have BB for battleship, CVA for attack aircraft carrier, CVU for plane transport, CVE for escort aircraft carrier, CLG for guided missile light cruiser, DDG for guided missile destroyer, ASSP for transport submarine, and so on down the battle line.

Our fliers, both military and commercial, have devised a process for aerial communications which may be described as abbreviations in reverse. If they need to spell out a word like France, they will give each letter a full word, thus: Foxtrot–Romeo–Alpha–November–Charlie–Echo. The rest of the alphabet runs as follows: Bravo, Delta, Golf, Hotel, India, Juliet, Kilo, Lima, Mike, Oscar, Papa, Quebec, Sierra, Tango, Uniform, Victor, Whisky,

X ray, Yankee, Zulu. But in the lingo of the fliers, Roger still means "received your message."

The same or a similar principle is employed by telephone operators when they wish to spell out a name (D for Dora, A for Alfred, Y for Yankee). But New York bopsters have devised a weird variant of this system which they apply to the names of telephone exchanges. In their "language," NEwtown becomes NErvous, FReeport becomes FRantic, and SUsquehanna becomes Crazy Man Crazy, for which there is no alphabetic justification whatsoever.

CHAPTER TWENTY-NINE

Names of Flags, Anthems, Currencies, Governing Bodies

Every duly constituted nation today sports a national flag, which is symbolical of the nation itself. The practice of having some form or other of symbolical insignia goes all the way back to the ancient Egyptians and Babylonians, and the Romans carried their wolf and their eagle all over the then known world.

Flags and standards bearing special identifying names arose in the Middle Ages, when the French kings carried into battle first the blue cloak of Saint Martin, later a banner device from the Abbey of Saint Denis to which the specific name of *Oriflamme* ("golden flame") was given. At a much later date, the flag of France became the famed *Fleur-de-Lis* ("lily flower"; three green lilies on a white background), which was symbolical of the French monarchy. The French Revolution changed to the *Tricolore* ("three colored"), consisting of three ver-

171

tical stripes of blue, white, and red. It is now sometimes adorned with De Gaulle's *Croix de Lorraine* ("cross of Lorraine").

Oldest among the national flags in existence today is the Danish (white cross on a red field), which goes back to the thirteenth century. The Danes poetically call it the *Dannebrog*, or "strength of Denmark."

The British Union Jack is symbolical of the union of England, Scotland and Ireland, its design combining the three crosses of Saint George, Saint Andrew and Saint Patrick. It is called a Jack because it is flown on the jackstaff of a war vessel.

Our own flag, which replaced the many state banners of the Revolution, is affectionately, but unofficially, termed the Stars and Stripes, descriptive of its appearance, or Old Glory. The South proudly displays by its side the Confederate Stars and Bars.

Many other national flags bear special names. The Italian *Tricolore* is patterned after the French. Many flags display a special symbol. Israel's bears the Star of David; India's flag, a newcomer, bears the Wheel of Asoka, one of the early Indian emperors; Morocco's flag shows the Seal of Solomon. The old Irish flag (not the one of the present Republic of Éire) bears "the harp that once through Tara's hall . . . ," while the present flag, bearing the constellation known as the Dipper, is sometimes referred to as "the Plough and the Stars." The swastika emblem appeared on the Nazi flag during Germany's Hitlerian regime, but has now vanished. The hammer and sickle device, or the five-pointed star, appears on the flag of most Communist countries.

National anthems are, like flags, symbolic of their countries, and are often known by a full-fledged title, usually taken from some line of their lyrics. In a few cases they bear what amounts to a specific individual name. This is true of the French *Marseillaise* (so called because it was sung during the French Revolution by volunteers from Marseille marching to defend Paris); the Belgian *Brabançonne* ("pertaining to the province of Brabant"); and the Israeli *Hatikwah* ("the hope"), which is a hymn to the return of the Jews to the Promised Land. Our *Star Spangled Banner* may also be said to fall into this class.

Side by side with the official national anthem there is often a popular patriotic song which supplements it, like our *America* and *Columbia the Gem of the Ocean*. Britain's official *God Save the King* (or *Queen*, depending on the sex of the ruling monarch) is accompanied by *Rule Britannia*. Canada's *The Maple Leaf Forever* is perhaps better known, at least south of the border, than the official Canadian anthem.

Changes of regime normally lead to changes both in national flags and national anthems. America, Britain and France have been fairly stable in this respect, at least since the end of the eighteenth century. Germany, on the other hand, shifted from an imperial anthem sung to the same tune as Britain's *God Save the King* and our own *America*, and flanked by such secondary anthems as *Die Wacht am Rhein* ("The Watch on the Rhine") and *Deutschland über Alles* ("Germany above Everything") to the *Horst Wessel Lied* under the Nazi regime (Horst Wessel was a Nazi leader who was killed before Hitler came to power). Italy, which had a *Marcia Reale* ("royal march"), flanked by a *Garibaldi Anthem*, practically shifted to *Giovinezza* ("youth") under Mussolini, and now has gone back to an old Mameli anthem, inherited from the days of the Italian wars for independence. Spain has fluctuated between the old *Marcha Real* ("royal march") and the *Himno de Riego*, a revolutionary song. Russia, which had in the days of the tsars a majestic anthem entitled *Bozhe Tsarya Khrani* ("God Save the Tsar"), parts of which appear in Tchaikovsky's "1812" and "Marche Slav" overtures, swung to *Da Zdravstvuyet Rossiya* ("Long Live Russia") under Kerensky, then to the Communist *Internationale* in the early days of the Soviet regime, and now has an anthem, or *Gimn* (this is the same word as "hymn," remembering that Russian shifts *h* to *g*), chosen by a contest among Soviet song writers.

It is perhaps opportune to stress that the inhabitants of other lands normally regard their flags and anthems with the same veneration with which we regard our own, and that if we find ourselves in their countries we should display the same respect for their symbols that we expect for ours. Standing when the national anthem is played and removing your hat when the flag passes by are international customs. This custom is abused in cases where both flag and anthem are made to serve the interests of a party or group, rather than those of a nation. Anti-Nazi Germans abhorred the Swastika emblem while it lasted, and anti-Fascist Italians refused to sing or play *Giovinezza* because these were the symbols of Nazism and Fascism, not of Germany and Italy.

In the case of most countries more or less democratically run, the names of the legislative bodies are straight translations either of our Senate and House of Representatives, or of the British Houses of Parliament (not, however, House of Commons and House of Lords), or of the French Senate and Chamber of Deputies. A few special names for legislative bodies appear, such as the Irish Dail Eireann, the Israeli Knesset, the Dutch States General, the Icelandic Althing, the Finnish Eduskunta, the Iranian Majlis. The Germans formerly had a Reichstag, and the Russians a Duma.

For currencies there is great variety. Our dollar has a name that comes from *Joachimsthaler*, after coins minted from silver mined in Bohemia's Joachimsthal (St. Joachim's Dale or Valley). It has many currencies named after it. So has the British pound (originally a pound of silver); the abbreviation, £, stands for the Latin word for pound, *libra*. The same Latin *libra* is at the root of the Italian and Turkish *lira*. The *franc*, used by France, Belgium, Switzerland and other countries, is the coin of the Franks. Spanish-speaking lands often have the *peso* or *peseta*, words which come from a Latin word for weight, but many Latin-American currencies bear other names: *boliviano* or *bolívar*, commemorating the South American liberator; *sucre*, in honor of another Latin-American fighter for independence; *colón*, in honor of Columbus; *balboa; córdoba, sol* ("sun"), even *lempira, guaraní* and *quetzal*, taken from the Indian languages. Brazil has the *cruzeiro*, named after the Southern Cross, and Portugal the *escudo* ("shield"). The German *mark* is duplicated by the Finnish *markka*. The "crown" idea appears in the *koruna* of Czechoslovakia and in the *krone* or *krona* of the Scandinavian countries. The "lion" comes to the surface in the Rumanian *leu* and the Bulgarian *lev*. The *gulden* of Holland and the *zloty* of Poland have to do with gold. The *drachma* of Greece comes from antiquity, and is the same word as our "dram." "Royal" appears in such currencies as *real, rial* and *riyal*, used in Middle Eastern countries. The *rupee* of India and the *rupiah* of Indonesia go back to a Sanskrit word for "silver." The *dinar* of Yugoslavia and some Arab countries goes back to the Latin *denarius*, a coin of the ancient Romans, which also appears in the "denier" of our hosiery manufacturers. The Russian *ruble*, the Japanese *yen*, the Chinese *yuan*, the Haitian *gourde*, the Hungarian *forint*, round out the picture.

For minor currency units, the state of affairs is simpler, because most countries divide their major unit into one hundred parts, and the root of our cent (Latin *centum*, "one hundred") appears in the French *centime*, the Spanish *céntimo* and *centavo*, the Italian *centesimo*, etc. A few other minor units, taken at random, are: the British farthing, penny, shilling and crown; the Scandinavian *öre*; the Indian *pies, pice* and *annas*; the Japanese *sen*; the Russian *kopek*.

CHAPTER THIRTY

The Names of Seasons, Months and Holidays

The entire civilized world has a concept of the four seasons, and names for them which vary in accordance with the individual language. While German has in its word for Spring (*Frühling*) the idea of "early," and in its Fall (*Herbst*) that of "harvest," the Romance languages prefer "first" in connection with Spring (*primavera, printemps*), and universally use the Latin-derived Autumn in preference to our Anglo-Saxon Fall. Russian uses the same word (*lyeto*) indifferently for "summer" and "year," and the Russian question "How old are you?" sounds like "How many summers have you?"

In the names of the months, the system devised by the Romans, which is the one we use, is fairly general, although it has interesting exceptions. Both Jews and Arabs divide the year into twelve months, but their names are altogether different from ours. The Czechs still use the old Slavic month names, with a *Srpen* that means "sickle" and a *Listopad* that means "leaf falling," but the Russians have a set of month names that are recognizably the same as ours. There were old Germanic names for the months, based, like the Slavic, on natural phenomena, and Charlemagne even tried to introduce them into the official calendar of his times, but the experiment failed. At the time of the French Revolution, an attempt was made to substitute natural phenomena names like *Brumaire*, "Foggy," and *Pluvieux*, "Rainy," for the old traditional names, but this did not last long, either.

The Roman system, which we use, has January after the god *Janus*, February after *Februa*, the purification festivals, March after *Mars*, April from the root of the verb "to open," May after the goddess *Maia*, June and July after two Roman clans, August after the Emperor Augustus. The rest of the names are numerical but their order is clear proof that the original Roman year started in March, not in January. September, October and November, which have, respectively, the roots of *septem*, "seven," *octo*, "eight" and *novem*, "nine," were evidently the seventh, eighth and ninth months, whereas today they are the ninth, tenth and eleventh. In reckoning dates, the Romans made use of a complicated system of *calends, ides* and *nones*, which were later discarded in favor of a simpler numerical system (though *calends* still appears in "calendar").

The names of the Roman and Germanic gods and goddesses which go into the English, German and Romance names of the days of the week have already appeared.

The Russians use a different arrangement, with only *subbota* corresponding to our "Sabbath" and the Romance words for Saturday.

The seven-day week is fairly general, but it is of interest that the day of rest, which is Sunday to the Christians and Saturday to the Jews, is Friday to the Moslems and Thursday to the Hindus.

Religious holidays are as numerous and varied as the world's religions. Thanksgiving is specifically American, having been devised on American soil, but Christmas is international, at least wherever there are Christians. What changes is the name. Our word (originally "Christ's Mass") is to be found in a few other languages, Dutch among them, but Romance speakers prefer words derived from the Latin *natalis*, "pertaining to the birth" (of Christ). This takes the form of *Natale* in Italian, *Natal* in Portuguese, *Noël* in French. Spaniards make a slight variant and call the holiday *Navidad* ("Nativity"). The German *Weihnachten* and the Scandinavian *Jul* (our "Yule") go back to other sources: the former is "Consecration Night," the latter is pagan. The name of Easter likewise goes back to pagan times and the pagan Spring festivals. Here the Romance languages prefer words derived from the Hebrew *Pesach* ("Passover"). French has *Pâques*, Italian *Pasqua*, Spanish *Pascua*; but Spanish often uses the plural *Pascuas* in the sense of "holidays" in general. The Slavic tongues make use of the word for "Resurrection" (in Russian it is *Voskreseniye*, which also means "Sunday").

Another religious festivity is that of the Epiphany, on February 6th. The French call it *la Fête des Rois* ("the feast of the kings"), referring to the three Wise Men, or three Kings from the East, who brought gifts of gold, frankincense and myrrh to the Infant Jesus. The Italians call it *Befana*, a corruption of the Greek *Epiphania*, which means a "showing or display" (the public display of the Infant Jesus for the adoration of kings and shepherds). To Italian children, *la Befana* is also an old woman who brings them gifts, after the fashion of our Santa Claus. Many nations that have a patron saint celebrate the saint's feast, as Ireland and the Irish everywhere mark Saint Patrick's Day, March 17th, as the great holiday.

Hebrew religious festivals include *Yom Kippur*, "the day of atonement"; *Rosh Hashanah*, or New Year's Day (literally, "the head of the year"); *Hanukkah*, or "dedication," popularly known in some Jewish communities as the Feast of the Lights; *Purim* and *Sukkoth*.

National holidays, too, abound. Our Independence Day is paralleled by France's Bastille Day (July 14th, commemorating the fall of the Bastille and the triumph of the French Revolution), Britain's Empire Day (the birthday of Queen Victoria, May 24th), Italy's Constitution Day (September 20th), Canada's Dominion Day (July 1st).

Corresponding to what we call legal holidays, the British have their bank holidays (days on which banks are closed). These do not quite coincide for all parts of the United Kingdom, such as England and Scotland, nor do ours (in the North there is widespread celebration of Lincoln's Birthday, in the South of Robert E. Lee's. Even Memorial Day is celebrated on different days in the North and the South). British holidays or semiholidays which always intrigue Americans by reason of their names are Maundy Thursday, Boxing Day and Guy Fawkes Day. The first means "commanded Thursday," and refers to the command issued by Christ to wash the feet of the beggars. The second relates to the custom of giving Christmas boxes to postmen and tradespeople on the first weekday after Christmas. The third is in commemoration of the failure of Guy Fawkes and his fellow-plotters in their attempt to blow up the House of Parliament.

Every nation has its interesting ways and customs and holidays. Every nation has its names, which are very meaningful to its citizens. The variety is infinite, and we have given only a few scattered samples.

All of these, however, are rooted in and stem from the basic unity of what a great American artist has called "The Family of Man." Under the multitude of forms and names that appear on the surface, there is the same underlying love of God, of country, of home and family.

The names we have described, no matter from what source, portray the same general, unmistakably human traits. Color, race, nationality, religion, are incidental. What is basic is the unity of mankind, in emotions, affections, aspirations and ambitions.

Index

183